STAND
at the Cross Roads

*A True Story of an Imperfect Woman
on an Unlikely Mission
with God, Who Never Let Go*

Hilda Hellums Baker with Chris Rogers

To my grandchildren:

Grace Anne Jennings

Justin Clayton Jennings

Rebecca Paige Olive

Matthew J Olive

James Michael Olive

Benjamin Declan Derr

Nathaniel Rush Baker

Penelope Jane Derr

"Don't let anyone look down on you because you are young, but set an example for the believers in speech, in life, in love, in faith and in purity."

1 Timothy 4:12 (NIV)

A portion of the proceeds from this book will be donated to Cross Roads to provide for continuing improvements in its facilities and ministry.

Most tombstones have two dates on them separated by a dash. One date is for when you were born, the other for when you die. Life is what happens in the dash.

Anonymous

TABLE OF CONTENTS

Markers in our Faith

Do you remember where you were on the morning of September 11, 2001? A dumb question, of course you do. How can you forget? I was getting ready to go to the office when Iris Martin called and said, "Turn on the TV."

There are times and places in our lives that serve as markers. We mark our memories by those times and events. A friend of mine, the Reverend Billy Armstrong, shared his experiences of being a volunteer chaplain helping in the aftermath of 9/11. As he spoke of his feeling of the presence of God, and of the presence of the spirits of the people who died amid such destruction, his message was so strong I had to go to New York myself.

It was July 2002, but the feeling of God's spirit and the spirits of those who died there still lingered in the air as I gazed through the chain link fence at the hole in the ground where the towers once stood. You can feel the power of God, because so many people's lives were changed in that place.

Just as we have markers in history that take up residence in our lives, we have places and events that mark our spiritual journeys. There is a plaque marking the place where John Wesley sat in Aldersgate Church in England, where he said, "my heart was strangely warmed." I know exactly where I was when God called me into ministry. Hilda Baker knows where she was when God called her to create a camp where the lives of youth and adults would be touched by God and changed.

I became the pastor of St. John's United Methodist Church in Rockdale in 2003. Several months after settling in, my youth director told me we needed to get prepared for Cross Roads. All my youth, their parents and counselors would have nothing of going anywhere else but to this little camp in the woods.

The first time I pulled down the drive to Cross Roads I was part of a caravan of teenagers going there for a fall retreat. And to be honest, I was not impressed. The camp I was used to had many buildings, several swimming pools, a few lakes, a game room, basketball courts, and a thirty foot-high climbing wall. There in the headlights ahead of me sat a smallish building and two small green cabins. That was it.

My youth counselors assured me the youth loved going there, and sure enough they were very excited, but I didn't get it. What was so great about this place?

What turned out to be so great about Cross Roads that weekend was not the buildings but the people. You could feel, see and even taste the love.

There is something magnetic about people who have trained their ear to hear God. There is something intriguing about people who have made bold steps in their lives to follow a call from God. They are pioneers of faith. To follow God's call, they step out of their normal everyday world and begin a whole new life wherever it may take them. People are drawn to such passionate faith like moths around a light bulb on a hot summer evening.

I feel the spirit of God when I go through the gate at Cross Roads, and I like to think it is also the spirit of all the people whose lives have been changed and are being changed as you read the story of faith in the pages that follow. If we were to place a plaque to mark the spots where the lives of men, women and youth were transformed at Cross Roads, we would be surrounded by names in, the conference room, the dining hall, the cabins, the chapel, the outdoor tabernacle, the prayer trail, the ropes course and everywhere in between.

As I look back at my many experiences now at Cross Roads, seeing young people's lives change and witnessing many people hear and follow their own calls to ministry while at the camp, I have come to find Cross Roads is a place of power.

In Matthew Jesus said, "he who has ears to hear, let him hear." We all need to sharpen our spiritual ears. This is a book that needs to be heard. I thank God for people like Hilda Baker, who answer God's call. It is through them that we are blessed.

Reverend John Warren, Pastor
St. John's United Methodist Church
Rockdale, Texas

In resolving our issues, are we doomed to repeat them over and over, to relive the same situation until we finally get it right?

CHAPTER 1

Dogwoods and Danger

I was finished with men. Done.

After four failed marriages, I had no interest in traveling that path again. So how did I arrive at this place, at this beautiful clearing, surrounded by a thousand dogwoods scenting the air with their delicate blossoms, standing in front of a minister and about to utter those two dangerous little words, "I do"?

That was March 29, 2003. Seven years earlier, I was wielding a machete near the same clearing, hacking down yaupon scrub.

A year before that, I was a forty-six-year-old suburban housewife, my life unraveling faster than a cheap suit. Miserable in my marriage, I sought from my church what I was missing at home and discovered meaning, as well as refuge, through the friendship and support of several small groups and then by volunteering with my church's youth program.

But looking back even farther, I see that God had been working on and with me since I was a child. As a nosy six-year-old, eavesdropping on my mom and her friend discussing death over morning coffee, I innocently asked, "If what Jesus said is true, why are you afraid?"

In high school I took an aptitude test that determined I should be a ranch foreman. Me, a city *girl*, born and raised in Houston?

True, I'd always loved the outdoors. We lived near Clay Road and Highway 6, which back then was the boondocks. I rode horseback all over that area, through pastures, down wooded trails. My best friend and I would ride together for hours. That's when I was happiest, exploring, roaming the countryside, yet it took thirty years and four marriages for me to finally grasp what God was telling me in that aptitude test.

Each failed marriage taught me a bit more about life, and the toughest one taught me the most. That situation should never have happened, but plenty of single moms will relate to it. A struggling mother supporting three kids, I was exhausted, hungry for adult companionship, and feeling vulnerable. He was my boss. He had no children. A wrong choice from the start, but only later did I realize exactly how wrong.

As my home life disintegrated, my Christian life bloomed. I watched the remarkable young people at my church express their faith every day, and not just on the t-shirts they wore to school. Like all kids, they listened to music nonstop, but their favorite music was praise-and-worship and Christian rock. They enthusiastically invited their school friends to church events, anxious to share what so excited them. I learned more from those amazing kids than they ever learned from me.

Discovering Community

My two youngest children, Jeremy, seventeen, Nina, fifteen, both members of the youth group, received love and support by hanging out with their church friends, support that carried them through some rough times at home. The adult volunteers, many of whom grew to be my dear friends, came through for me in ways they never realized.

2

Our youth program's mission was to provide fellowship, build faith-forming relationships, learn to live life abundantly, and to worship passionately. Although I'd always known intellectually that Jesus is there for us, I'd never grasped that one way He accomplishes this feat is by working through people. In guiding me to volunteer with the youth program, He gave me the opportunity to learn. I was learning what I taught as I taught it. Yet as I coached these kids to be open, trusting, accepting, and to seek support and guidance from other Christians, I felt like a complete fraud.

The fear of being rejected by my new friends was so overwhelming that I couldn't open my own heart and trust that they would understand. I couldn't share the burden of my unhappy home life. In the face of these painful circumstances, the time I spent at church was like being in the eye of a storm, a safe and tranquil place in the midst of my chaotic life. My husband and I tried everything to make the marriage succeed, including years of counseling with several therapists, but when a situation never should have happened, patching it never works.

I escaped to the community of church. Our youth ministry took me out of the house, out of the prison I had created for myself, and gave me positive work to do, and my kids went with me. We took trips, mission trips, retreat trips, and we had a ball. Whether we were painting a house with Smurf blue paint in Baldwin, Louisiana, or digging outhouses in the Appalachians, we had fun. The kids loved it. I loved it. We felt accepted and useful. We felt loved. We felt at peace.

The day we returned from our mission trip to the Appalachian Mountains in Tennessee marked the moment I knew my marriage was over. We went there to repair homes, build wheelchair ramps and yes, dig outhouses in solid rock. We worked our tails off during the daytime hours. At night we slept in tents in the national forest. Doing God's work, you can't help feeling good about yourself. When we arrived back at the church parking lot, everyone else's family had come to welcome us home and affirm us for doing a good job, but my husband wasn't there.

The kids and I drove home that day laughing as we relived our adventure, but a cloud of apprehension about what lay ahead of us dampened our high spirits. Nervously, I pressed the button on the garage door opener and as the door went up it revealed my husband standing there, screaming at us for being two hours late.

I saw the handwriting on the wall. My kids did not deserve his constant bullying, and neither did I. Nevertheless, it would be several months before the marriage finally collapsed.

For six years following the divorce, I had no interest in men. I didn't date. My focus turned toward the path I knew Christ wanted me to take. I created a new life doing the work He wanted me to do on a Christian youth retreat, miles from anything I knew, a work still in progress today. Despite a continuous string of physical and financial challenges, I felt as happy as when I was horseback riding with my friend in the Houston boondocks.

So how did I end up, on March 29, 2003, in a clearing of yaupon and dogwoods, standing beside a man my best friend had told me to avoid like poison ivy, a man who once thought of me as a Holy Roller, a man I once considered a heathen?

"Do you take this man …?"

God doesn't choose the qualified, He qualifies the chosen.

CHAPTER 2

God's Guideposts: Learn as You Go

I knew nothing about using a chainsaw, but God placed one in my hands anyway. I knew nothing about moving a house, but God gave me one to move, and boy, did I fail that test, at least the first time around. Before doing that, however, He gave me 160 acres, thick with yaupon scrub and thorny greenbrier vines. He intended to use me to clear the land and build a retreat.

In preparation, many, many years before that, He gave me three beautiful children to nurture and mold. Has any mother ever hit a perfect score on that job? If so, she should be sainted.

No blueprint, no guidelines. Much of the time I had no help. My own childhood certainly didn't prepare me for motherhood.

Outsiders

In 1948, when my parents met at Tarleton Junior College, they had a lot in common. They both felt like outsiders. My mother's favorite poem, she once told me, characterized their relationship. I remember only one line, but that single line says it all: *He built a wall around his heart and wouldn't let me in, so I built my wall around it all and gladly took him in.* My mom spent most of her life and energy trying to break down that wall, while Dad spent his time and energy working to achieve the American dream, which he did quite admirably. There just didn't seem to be much left to share with their kids.

My mother and her identical twin sister lost their mother shortly after birth and were placed in an orphanage, where they lived for two years before being adopted. This was during the Great Depression. Although their new family was large, extended, and wealthy, I don't believe my mother ever felt completely accepted. During the school year, she had a nanny, who dressed her up every evening to visit briefly with her parents before dinner. Children ate separately, except on special occasions. Considering her childhood circumstances, my mother undoubtedly did the best she could with her own children, and I know she loved us dearly, but I never felt like she quite knew how to deeply connect with us.

The story's told that the town rang the firehouse bell the day my dad was born. He was the fifth child, and first son, of a prominent West Texas businessman who died when my dad was only thirteen. My grandmother was left to run the family grocery store; so much of my dad's parenting fell to his older sisters. Dad's mother, before she married, was a schoolteacher who drove her horse-drawn buggy all over the county tutoring the children of local ranchers. Both his parents were staunch Presbyterians.

Growing up in their separate extraordinary circumstances, my parents had little guidance in creating healthy parent-child relationships. The oldest of five children, and often in charge of my siblings, I was never taught what to do or how to handle the basics of everyday living, I was simply expected to know. As a family, we attended church together only until I was old enough to drive. Then I took the other kids to church. We were left to figure out life on our own, much like my parents were.

So my early years were pretty much "learn as you go." Whatever problem came up, I was expected to know how to deal with it.

I didn't.

The day after I graduated from high school, my family left me completely on my own and moved to Scotland. I couldn't balance a checkbook. I didn't know how to handle money. I was clueless about surviving as an adult, and I was set up for failure.

From the Mouths of Babes

Right away, I failed at college, dropping out before the end of my first semester. I also dropped out of church. Two years later, I married for the first time, and failed at that. My husband, Bill never settled into married life. A year into the marriage I became pregnant, and the added responsibility was too great for him. He left, so, at the age of twenty-three, I found myself a divorced single mother.

If we listen, children have a way of teaching us what we need to know. Jennifer and I grew up together. She was a beautiful, energetic, high-spirited child, and while I often felt overwhelmed, I cherished her. Light brown hair, emerald eyes, and rosy cheeks: she has her father's Irish good looks.

I worked for a big brokerage firm in downtown Houston, as an underwriting assistant for the municipal bond department. I did well at that, but Jennifer and I struggled through some tough times. When she was about five, I met my brother's roommate, Bob, a crazy man but a lot of fun. Bob and I hit it off, and I married for the second time. We moved to Austin, built our dream house in the Texas hill country, and opened our own business. We had some really good years together. Jeremy, a tow-headed, blue-eyed, perpetual motion machine, came along during those good times. Then the Jimmy Carter era hit, with high interest rates. Our business failed, so we had to sell our house and move back to

Houston, into a rental. Nina, my third child and a carbon copy of her brother, was born shortly afterward.

Jennifer, the social butterfly of the family, soon met our next-door neighbors, who also had a little girl. Heather and Jennifer, both eight years old, became best friends. Heather's family went to church every Sunday morning and Wednesday night, and when Heather invited Jennifer to go to Sunday school with her, I said, "Sure."

My, did that open a floodgate. Jennifer bombarded me with endless questions.

"Why don't we have a church, Mom? Why don't we go to church? Don't you like church? I like church. We can go to Heather's church. Why won't you come to Heather's church with me?" She never stopped.

Finally, I said, "Okay!"

My eight-year-old daughter had shamed me back to church and back toward God.

Trials, Tests and Fortitude

Perhaps Jennifer was my first guidepost, turning me toward my mission. Once I was back in, of course, I was all in. Our minister, Reverend Ozzie Lutz, taught me more about the Bible than I'd ever known in my life. So grace-filled and so full of love, he was a wonderful mentor. Eventually, I became an elder in the Presbyterian Church, my first experience in a leadership role. When Ozzie retired, and we needed a new minister, I served on the Pastor Search Committee and learned that I'm not cut out for church politics.

Jennifer was fifteen when Bob and I divorced. This time it was circumstances that killed the marriage. The 1980s oil and gas crisis crashed the Texas economy, and after our business failed, Bob lost his bearings. We did manage to buy a house in

Houston, but times were tough, and we got behind in our mortgage payments. I needed to take a job, but finding employment that brought in enough to make a difference after we paid for childcare proved impossible. This must have added to Bob's distress. When we received an eviction notice, with thirty days to move out, I told him we *had* to do something. We couldn't continue ignoring our predicament. I called my dad, who had a rent house a few miles away, and asked what he would charge us to live there.

"Move in," he said, after I described my predicament in detail. "We'll discuss the money later."

For Bob, that was the last straw. He walked out and didn't look back.

I packed up our things, called some men from the church to help, and we moved into my parents' rent house. Shortly afterward, my pastor helped me get a job with an insurance agency.

Jennifer, however, was at a pivotal age, and I believe the financial stress and emotional turmoil of those years marked the beginning of her rebellion.

I've heard that raising kids is a lot like playing golf, a hit-or-miss proposition. You keep hoping you're going to get it right. What I didn't realize at the time was that living through the trials of my daughter's teenage years developed in me the fortitude I would need later when He set me on the path He intended me to walk.

Love Hurts

Sixteen is not an easy age. When I was sixteen, my parents accused me of sort of every sort of misconduct, from drinking and running wild to sleeping with my boyfriend, and I had done none of it. I was so good, so well behaved, that I could've been a poster child for "just say no." But that didn't convince my dad.

9

Six-foot-one, medium build, trim and quite handsome, my dad was a self-made man. At work, Dad commanded a tremendous amount of authority, and at home his word was law, at least where the children were concerned. One day I came home a little late from who knows where, and my dad once again accused me of something I hadn't done. Sick of being wrongly accused, I spouted off.

"Well, you're just wrong," I told him.

He slapped me. This was the first time he'd ever slapped me.

I slapped him back.

Dad looked at me like I had two heads, but he never again touched me, and we had a new understanding from that point forward.

I'm not proud of what happened that day, but he was wrong. And at sixteen, I was learning to stand up for what's right. That part of my character, which frequently gets me in trouble, has never changed.

When I was seventeen, Dad was transferred to Scotland. He went ahead of the family to get things ready. We were left behind with Mom to finish up the school year, my senior year. She inherited the job of selling the house, getting me into college, and moving the rest of the household overseas. It was a turbulent, chaotic, nonsensical year. I remember one particular evening that deteriorated into Mom and I wrestling on the floor over something as ridiculous as feeding the dog.

When Jennifer rebelled at sixteen, she acted on most of the unruly teenage offenses I was accused of doing at that age but never had. Alcohol, drugs, I wasn't sure what she did during those times she thwarted my efforts to keep her at home, but I knew she needed help. The first time Jennifer ran away, I found her at the apartment of a boy she'd been dating. The next time, because

I was "too strict", she stole my car and ran away to my parents' house, and they wouldn't let me have her back.

My father and mother, who had their own hands full with my teenage sister, were telling me I was wrong to want my daughter to stop sabotaging her life. I was taking things to seriously. I was an evil witch because I wanted to put her in rehab, yet I only wanted to fix this thing that had gone so terribly wrong. Because Jennifer was sixteen, the police said I couldn't force her to leave her grandparents' home, unless she was a danger to herself or others.

"She's definitely a danger to herself," I told them.

"Then here's what you'll need to do…." They wanted me to make sure Jennifer would be at my parent's house when they arrived to pick her up.

All day, I walked around nauseated, with a huge knot in my stomach, probably approaching a nervous breakdown. Once I tried dialing a number that I'd called countless times, I couldn't remember it. My hands trembled. I was scared to death.

I drove alone to my parents' house. The police had told me where to wait.

"When you see us drive up," they said, "walk in behind us."

As I followed them in, I saw my dad and mom sitting in their car. Dad rolled the window down as I passed by.

"What the hell have you done?"

The bitterness in his voice reminded me of all the unwarranted accusations I'd heard from him growing up. A streak of steely determination shot down my back.

With my knees about to give way, I looked him straight in the eyes and said, "I've handled it."

I walked past them into the house.

The police arrested Jennifer, snapped handcuffs on her, placed her in the squad car right in front of my parents, and drove her to Charter Hospital.

That event was a huge turning point for us. Jennifer will tell you now that I saved her life that night. But at the time, she was furious. My daughter was safe, however, and for me that was all that mattered.

Despite believing I was right in taking control of that volatile situation, it was one of the hardest tasks God has ever given me. Little did I know it was only one of many to come.

If you're paying attention, you can see God at
work. You can feel Him all around.

CHAPTER 3

His Voice

"Surely there must be a place we could've gone that was closer than this," I murmured, sick of the endless bus ride, the sweltering heat, the exuberant antics and periodic bickering going on throughout the bus.

Who could blame the kids, though, for being keyed up? They were hot and tired, too, with their own boisterous way of expressing it.

"We looked everywhere," said one of the other volunteers. "This is the only retreat facility nearby that's both private *and* affordable."

A five-hour drive on the interstate and now this dark, winding country road, you call that nearby? Middle of summer, no air conditioning. Why had I expected this trip to be fun?

But she was right. Christian retreats were usually planned denominational events that brought together youth from many different member churches. Our youth director wanted a private retreat so we could deal with some issues that had arisen in the group. We rented a couple of school buses to haul forty kids, six counselors, a ton of teenage luggage, and a mountain of snacks and sodas on our trek south. Tardy teens caused us to get a late start. When we stopped for dinner the kids scattered like ants between three neighboring fast food establishments. Recapturing them delayed us even further.

"Where are we now?" someone piped. "On the road to nowhere?"

"It's nearly midnight," came another voice. "Are we ever going to stop?"

The endless drive finally ended. I peered out the bus window and, scattered among the trees, could barely make out some buildings. They looked pretty grim, not at all reassuring.

No outdoor lighting. No one to greet us. The caretakers had obviously given up and gone to bed.

Our fearless leader rose from her seat.

"Wait here. Let me see if I can find someone." She headed for the exit as the bus driver opened the doors.

The kids didn't wait. Whooping and cheering, they clamored off the bus. After being cooped up for five hours, they were not about to be contained any longer.

"Where's a bathroom?" a girl asked on her way out the door.

"And the food!" asked a boy bouncing anxiously behind her.

As they spilled noisily into the night, our frantic leader told the bus driver to honk the horn and let someone, anyone, know that we'd arrived.

After a few minutes, a middle-aged couple emerged haggardly from the shadows. They hustled over to us, seeming a bit perturbed by our late arrival. It was soon clear that we weren't the first to drag them from their beds at midnight to check in. They led us to a small, shabby meeting room.

Inside, they pointed out two doors. "Boys to the right, girls to the left. You'll find bathrooms, showers, and dormitories with bunks."

The kids ran excitedly to check out their new territories. Seconds later, the girls' shrieks sent us scurrying to see what was wrong. I expected an animal of some kind had found its way inside the dorm, or maybe a nest of giant hairy spiders.

But it wasn't a presence that had upset them. It was an absence, a complete absence of comfort anywhere, and a complete absence of privacy for bathing. The ten showers had no partitions: communal bathing at its most rustic. PVC pipe glued together formed overhead circles that hung parallel from the ceiling. The intention, apparently, had been to hang shower curtains to encircle the space in front of each showerhead, but no curtains had been hung.

The plywood wall dividing the showers from the dorms was cracked and peeling. There were few windows and a few rattling ceiling fans, but no air conditioning.

A rank smell emanated from somewhere. Later, we traced it to the plastic mattresses. We imagined it was mildew, and hoped that's all it was. We never did figure it out.

"This can't be it," one of the girls wailed, mascara streaking her cheeks as the tears rolled.

I felt like crying right along with her. Here we were in South Texas in the heat of summer, on what was supposed to be an enjoyable weekend of community and renewal. The interminable bus ride had taken its toll on all of us, and now our destination was a disaster. Strike two for the retreat "experience."

My gaze traveled from one tear-stained girl to the next. The shock was palpable.

But what could we do? By then, it was well past midnight of a very long day. Even a smelly bed was better than another five-hour drive on that bus.

The Fresh Mood of Dawn

Saturday morning broke to the aroma of frying bacon and coffee. Sweaty night or not, none of the girls had any interest in showering, and neither did the boys. We piled through the door ahead of schedule looking for the source of the delicious aromas.

It didn't take long to zero in on the dining hall. The caretakers, recovering their good spirits and joined by their teenage daughter, had obviously been up for quite a while preparing breakfast. As we passed through the food line, the family served up smiles along with heaping plates of fluffy pancakes and sizzling sausage, with cereal for those who wanted lighter fare. The tensions of the previous night began to fade.

After breakfast the couple pulled up a bench and sat at our table. Good-natured chitchat: *How was your trip? How long did it take? How did you sleep?* soon turned to questions about their ministry. They were obviously overwhelmed by the job, and money was in short supply. The man functioned as caretaker, they told us, while the woman ran the kitchen. Their daughter cheerfully helped when and where she was needed. With some prodding the couple continued to share the story of the camp. As they spoke they became more and more animated, their eyes shone with their love for Christ and the camp ministry.

As we emerged from the dining hall, on that hot South Texas morning, our stomachs pleasantly full and our own good spirits restored, we saw what the dark had hidden from us the previous night. Huge oak trees shaded the benches, swings, and picnic tables that dotted the landscape. A charming gazebo framed a small fire pit. Hand-painted markers pointed the way to trails that wound through the woods. The kids, eager to explore, dashed ahead.

Following a trail, we found a creek nearby, replete with canoes but with a sign bearing a stern warning: NO SWIMMING OR WADING. The creek, the sign explained, was full of alligator gar.

In Texas, if you live anywhere near freshwater lakes, creeks or rivers, you know that unlike other gars, a gator gar has a double row of large, sharp teeth. The teeth, along with its long snout and olive color, give the fish its name. Also like real alligators, the gator gar can breathe air and, for a couple of hours, survive out of the water.

The boys instantly bared their teeth, curled their fingers into claws and began terrorizing the girls. The girls squealed with pretend fear. For a retreat that only a few hours ago had seemed a dismal failure, things were looking up.

Accidental Learning

We claimed the gazebo for our morning devotional. Sitting in a circle, with our youth director leading us in prayer, the retreat regained it's spiritual intent. Afterward, we broke into small groups. Each counselor had prepared a lesson based on a scripture for his or her group to discuss. The discussions were about learning to live and work together, to accept one another with all our faults and weaknesses. We'd been experiencing some infighting among the group; certain kids were being left out, no one wanting to sit beside them on the bus, that sort of thing.

When the program began, everybody joined in singing, whether they could carry a tune or not, followed by skits and teambuilding games. Then we read and discussed the scripture lesson, and most of the kids shared stories.

After lunch, the kids had free time, while the counselors took turns napping. We knew the evening would stretch long into the night.

In the afternoon, we challenged the kids to put together the evening worship. Delighted, they spread out around the grounds, each group responsible for a portion of the program, which commenced after dinner. The kids had done a splendid job. Plenty of music, and I was surprised at how thoughtfully they'd worked to come up with meaningful prayers and scriptures.

To wind down before bedtime, we lit the fire that the gentleman caretaker had laid in the gazebo pit and gathered around it. Even in hot weather, a blazing fire is always a big part of a retreat. Something about sitting around a campfire at night quiets the soul and brings out a person's introspective side. More than entertainment, it draws people together, out of the darkness, out of themselves as they sit by side mesmerized by the flickering flames. The day's activities had definitely brought the group closer in spirit. They'd worked together harmoniously, they were beginning to relax and the walls were melting in the warmth of the campfire.

A big part of it, I realized, was taking them out of their comfort zones, away from their home and school activities, away from computers, games, and televisions. That's the beauty of a retreat, all that naturally quiet space. When you cut down on the static, God can get through.

Around the crackling campfire, eating S'Mores or engaged in a "Chubby Bunny" contest to see who could cram the most marshmallows in their mouths, I watched these kids bond ever closer to one another, making friends for life. By the time we returned to the dorms, the sleeping and bathing facilities no longer seemed a hindrance. Still chatting about their day and their plans for tomorrow, the girls cheerfully held up towels for each other so they could shower modestly.

But one girl in particular, who had problems at school and had been acting out for weeks, needed our attention. Loud, occasionally obnoxious, she *always* needed to be the center of attention.

"The others just don't like me," she whined.

"Well, let's talk about that," we suggested. And that we did, staying up till the wee hours, talking with her, counseling her, and praying with her. She was upset and not feeling good about herself. It was an emotional night for all of us, but we worked through it together.

჻ஒ ஒ჻

Sunday morning started early. Awake long before schedule, the kids were ready to get on with their day. We sat on the swings, visiting and enjoying the fragrant country air, the morning breeze still cool enough to be comfortable, until the caretakers clanged a huge bell summoning us to the dining hall for breakfast. The kids gulped their food and took off outside, while the counselors visited with the staff before the Sunday morning devotionals.

More small-group discussions were followed by more free time. Soon after lunch, we'd be boarding the buses to leave, so the kids needed to let loose any excess energy. It was during this free time that we heard screams coming from the creek.

The girl we'd stayed up with the night before had taken a canoe out on the lake, alone, and capsized it, some said intentionally. For her, a warning sign served as an invitation to defy it. Naturally, she became a tempting target for an alligator gar.

Kids, adults, caretakers, we all rushed to help. Two boys fished her out of the lake. A couple more carried her back to the dorms, the whole crowd following, chattering, worried about her. I couldn't help wondering if this was exactly what she had wanted to happen.

What really struck me, though, was the way all the kids jumped forward to help this girl who'd been a thorn in their sides for weeks. A girl who whined and complained and created trouble at every opportunity. A girl nobody wanted to sit beside on the bus. After only two days at this retreat, in this incredibly rustic and revitalizing environment, the others were caring for her as they would care for a friend, as they would for any other member of the group.

If you're paying attention, I thought, you can see God at work here. You can feel Him all around.

The Eyes of My Heart Opened

I'd been on mission trips before, and years earlier I'd gone on a women's retreat, but none of them had impacted me like this one. This, in the late summer of 1995, was my first youth ministry retreat, and it awakened in me a passion that continues burning to this day. I determined long before the weekend was over that it would not be my last youth retreat.

On that Sunday morning, shortly before departure time, I found myself despondent about returning home. Freshly showered, I sat on a wide swing suspended from the massive arm of an oak tree, watching clusters of teens scattered across the grounds, playing games, singing praise-and-worship songs as one of the group strummed along on a guitar, or just talking and listening and being there for one another other. I wondered how many of them realized the gift they'd been given, the gift of being a part of this loving community of faith, the gift of not having to figure out life all by themselves. I wondered how many of them realized that despite the rough start and rudimentary accommodations, this was a little taste of heaven.

It wasn't about the place. It was about experiencing God and life together.

At home, my life was dead-on-course for a train wreck. My third husband and I understood the crux of our problem. Much of it stemmed from my need to develop my own identity. A business would give me the freedom to be me. Steve, my husband, didn't understand that need any more than my parents had when I was a child. Every time I found an idea that excited me, he jumped in and took it over. I was right back where I started, stifled, depressed and resentful.

Sitting on that swing, I thought, *it's not going to work out. It just isn't.* I looked around at the kids and realized that the only time I was ever at peace was on a trip with the youth group. The thought of going home filled me with dread. *What am I going to do?* I asked Him. *I know you don't want me living in misery. I know you've got something better planned for my life. What do you want me to do?*

From my earliest memories, I'd always felt that God had a purpose for me to fulfill. Although I had no clue what it might be, I sensed that my purpose would someday become clear. In junior and senior high school, I was an avid reader of biographies, little blue books about Annie Oakley, Marie Curie, and other courageous people. *If they can do these wonderful, positive, useful things with their lives,* I wondered, *why can't I? Is something wrong with me?*

Sitting there beneath the oak trees, the thought occurred to me that if I could do anything in the world for the rest of my life, this would be it: Provide a place where God can break through the chaos of everyday life to touch, change, and empower lives. Watching the kids this weekend experiencing their spirituality at a deeper level than most adults experience in a lifetime, a striking revelation had hit me. Most camps I'd ever heard of were missing the point, with their swimming pools, basketball courts, and all the latest, jazziest equipment for entertaining kids. Those same distractions existed in the kids' everyday lives. Here, in this minimal, unsophisticated camp, they had experienced the joy of living in a community of faith.

What might have changed in my life had I experienced God in this way at an early age? I realized then that I would give anything to help save one child, one person, from the pain of making some of the mistakes I'd made.

A feeling welled up from deep inside me. Like a tidal wave, it swelled and flooded my senses, overtaking me completely. As

John Wesley once said, "my heart was strangely warmed". The sensation subsided imparting absolute mental clarity.

It was then that I felt God speak. "You can do this. I will be with you."

His words were crystal clear, unmistakable, and electrifying as they resonated within me. In that transformative moment of clarity and surety, I was changed forever.

I knew absolutely that what I had envisioned would eventually happen. I didn't know how, when, where, or what would have to transpire, but I knew that if I trusted God He would use me to get it done.

In the wake of His words, I experienced a peace that surpasses all understanding, an incredible serenity, spent, as if I'd shed a bucket of tears. But I was dry eyed and smiling.

I smiled for the rest of the trip.

> *"Our deepest fear is not that we are inadequate. Our deepest fear is that we are powerful beyond measure. It is our light, not our darkness, that most frightens us. We ask ourselves, who am I to be brilliant, gorgeous, talented and fabulous? Actually, who are you not to be? You are a child of God. Your playing small doesn't serve the world. There is nothing enlightened about shrinking so that other people won't feel insecure around you. We were born to manifest the Glory of God that is within us."*
>
> – by Marianne Williamson from A Return To Love: Reflections on the Principles of A Course in Miracles

A coincidence? I don't think so! Where God guides He provides.

CHAPTER 4

The Search

All the way home my soul soared with excitement. Ideas, possibilities, and fears bounced around inside my head like pinballs.

"What would you think about having a retreat like that of our own?" I asked Jeremy and Nina.

"Really? That'd be great!"

"And we could go there any time? Yea!"

Even though Steve and I had been contemplating the possibility of my starting a business, I had no idea how he'd react to building a youth retreat from scratch. On the long drive home, I called Jennifer and tested the idea on her. She was supportive, thought it was a great idea, exactly what I needed, but she was also quiet. An hour or so later, she called me back.

"Mom, if you do this, if you decide to go ahead with this retreat idea, Scott and I want to help. We want to be part of it."

I was stunned. They'd only been married a year. They lived in Dallas, where Jennifer taught fourth grade and Scott had a job in advertising and marketing with a high-powered magazine. But if they wanted to help bring this dream together, then we could certainly move faster. Of course, I still had to convince Steve.

One thing Steve and I shared was our church life, so I figured he'd at least listen when I told him about my experience at the retreat.

"God put it on my heart to do this. I've thought about it all the way home, and I believe this would be a really cool business idea for us." It was obvious that I believed in what I was saying.

He was all for it. He loved the idea of owning the land. So when I mentioned buying some real property, he got excited. We talked about it being a project we could start now and pull together a little at a time, a great idea for a kind of "working" retirement plan.

"I don't know what God has in mind," I said, "about when or how or what needs to transpire, but why don't we start looking for some property?"

Immediately, I initiated a property search. Drawing on my experience of that long ride to South Texas, I knew that for a weekend retreat, an hour and a half was the ideal length of time you'd want to spend on a Friday night with a band of exuberant teenagers. Far enough away to feel that you've ventured outside the city, far from your normal routines and comforts, but close enough to make the trek enjoyable.

Sitting at my kitchen table with a Texas map and a compass, I marked a ninety-mile radius around Houston. I telephoned the various chambers of commerce for each county within the circle, asking for the names of local realtors, jotting their numbers on a notepad, and then began the tedious task of calling them.

"I'm looking for about fifty acres of undeveloped land." I didn't mention building a Christian retreat. The memory of the 1993 tragedy involving David Koresh and his ill-fated followers was still fresh in the minds of most Texans. The concept of a retreat, a simple, natural environment that encourages a communion with God, no matter what spiritual discipline you choose, is the furthest thing from what Koresh was doing. A retreat opens its doors to all, but only for short visits. Amazingly, people confuse the two concepts.

Acreage within ninety miles of Houston brought premium dollar, I soon learned. The oil and gas boom in Grimes County had caused property values to skyrocket. Washington County, with its picturesque rolling hills, attracted both Houstonians and Austinites to expensive country-home getaways. In fact, on any given Friday afternoon the exodus of Houstonians escaping the city created bumper to bumper traffic in all directions, which could stretch a pleasant ninety-minute jaunt into a nerve-wracking three-hour drive. Whether south toward the coast, north or east toward the lakes, or west to the hill country, I couldn't find a single piece of property in any of the counties I queried that fell within our price range.

As frustration set in, I imagined our project crashing before it even got off the ground. I sat stewing over it when Jeremy came in and looked over my shoulder at the map.

"Hey! That's Caldwell," he exclaimed. "Margaret lives there. And it's in your circle."

Margaret had been Jeremy's "summer romance" at Camp ChoYeh one summer. He was right, Burleson County, including the town of Caldwell, sat on the farthest northwest edge of the perimeter I'd drawn. Incredibly, it was almost dead center between Austin, Waco, Houston, and San Antonio. An ideal location. Traveling northwest from Houston, the Friday traffic would be tolerable, and a new stretch of highway was almost complete.

Anxious, knowing I was running out of feasible options, I called the Burleson County Chamber of Commerce. The woman named five realtors. Looking over the list, I chose one, said a prayer and dialed. I told the gentleman who answered what I was looking for.

He hemmed and hawed a bit, then said, "I've got this one piece of property, but it's more acreage than you want. Can't run cows on it, can't grow anything on it, and it's completely covered in oak trees and yaupon thickets. It ain't good for nothin', but it's cheap."

When he told me the price, I gasped. We didn't need 160 acres, but who could turn it down? He quoted $500 an acre, as opposed to the $5,000 an acre I'd heard from every other realtor. Was it too good to be true?

Or was it, God's hand guiding me, again?

Needless to say, Steve and I loaded up the car that very morning and headed to the tiny town of Chriesman, just north of Caldwell, to check it out. A chilly February afternoon found us driving down a winding country road lined intermittently by fenced pastures, wooded stretches, and an occasional house. You wouldn't think a property with half a mile of frontage would be hard to find, but the tangled thicket of trees, greenbrier vines, and underbrush along the fence line obliterated the tiny FOR SALE sign. After much driving back and forth, we located the correct worthless tract of land. Actually seeing the land proved impossible.

What was back there behind the impenetrable wall of growth? Swamp land? A local garbage dump? Or only more of the same jungle that confronted us? An aerial map supplied by the realtor showed faint outlines of dry creek beds, the remnants of an overgrown logging road, and two clearings that had apparently been oil well locations, but if all that were truly hidden in there you'd never know it.

After trying fruitlessly for an hour or so to find an inroad to explore, we noticed a woman across the street inspecting a house that was under construction. We drove over to introduce ourselves. Faye Cook and her husband, Don, after having successful careers in Austin, were moving back to Chriesman and building a new home on her ancestral land. When we asked what she knew about the mysterious property across the street, Faye told us that she believed a widow had owned the land. When the widow passed away, she left the property to the Moody Bible Institute in Chicago. Dwight L. Moody, who was always a step ahead of the status quo, founded the college in 1886 to train and empower women, to reach out to lost children, and to bridge the gap between denominations.

I felt goose bumps all over my body. A coincidence? I don't think so!

"Thank You, God," I murmured.

Fish or Cut Bait

All the way home, Steve and I discussed the possibilities. I saw only positive aspects: location, price, and availability. Sure, we might find some unusable areas behind the fence line, but with so much property, there had to be at least one perfect spot for our purposes. This was where God wanted the retreat to be built. I was sure of it.

Steve, however, felt extremely leery of buying that much property sight unseen. He needed more than the aerial photograph and topographical survey map to prove it wasn't a worthless tract. He needed to see for himself what was beyond that impenetrable growth. Plus, this was February, not the prettiest time of year for leafless deciduous trees.

"What are the odds that the first place we looked at is owned by the Moody Bible Institute?" I asked my husband. "It's a God thing! We have to have trust Him and step forward."

He shook his head. "We need to think about this."

Undeterred by his apprehension, when we arrived home I called the realtor.

"Another buyer, who intends to develop a subdivison, is also looking at the property," he cautioned.

"We plan to build a Christian retreat," I said, revealing this for the first time. "It's called Cross Roads. Youth groups from all over central Texas will come and spend weekends there. That seemingly "worthless" property is just the kind of material God likes to work with. It's perfect."

When the realtor called the Moody Bible Institute with our offer, and they learned our plans for the land, they dropped the price by one hundred dollars an acre.

Incredible. At that price, we couldn't pass it up. Steve finally had to admit that perhaps God did have His hand on our shoulders.

When we returned to sign the papers, Steve and the realtor shook hands. After we were outside again, I said, "I can't believe that went so smoothly."

"Well, he's a Mason."

"How do you know that?"

"I could tell by his handshake."

"So that means you're a Mason?"

Steve brushed it off, but I realized then that I'd just learned something about my husband that he'd never disclosed in our ten years of marriage. I didn't actually know anything about Masons, but if sharing that designation made Steve feel more comfortable with the realtor, more comfortable buying the property I knew God intended us to have, then I was all for it.

The day was bright, and crisp and joyous.

"Thank You, God." I whispered again, wiping the tears rolling down my cheeks.

Disentangling

Jennifer and Scott couldn't wait to see the property they might soon be living on. After talking it over, they were enthusiastically ready to leave their jobs in Dallas and put their full-time efforts into making Cross Roads a reality. For Steve and I, their commitment was another Godsend. We couldn't leave Houston, where our business provided our bread and butter plus the money to invest in Cross Roads, and overseeing such a large construction project from afar would have been difficult.

Jeremy and Nina were absolutely elated about the prospect of having a place in the country. So the following weekend, we all met beside the imposing courthouse anchoring the center of Caldwell's town square and, together, we made the ten-mile trek out to Chriesman. We spent a wonderful afternoon hacking trails through the heavy foliage, looking for the old logging road shown on the aerial photo. But after hours of tireless exploring, we still had absolutely no idea of where it was or what the land we were buying contained.

Undaunted, we returned to our respective homes, changed our focus, and began putting together a comprehensive business plan. We checked out "How To" books from the library. A friend of ours volunteered to draw the blueprints for a conference center. Scott helped him with the materials lists and handled the marketing survey.

Unfortunately, the hope of this retreat project bringing my husband and I closer together evaporated like morning fog. The ensuing weeks and months became increasingly difficult at home. For me, the retreat was an extension of the church activities that had held me together for a number of years. At church, I was appreciated, loved, supported, empowered, and most of all respected. This wasn't true at home. I soaked up the affirmation offered by my Christian friends, and this change in me met with ever increasing hostility from my husband.

I had worked with Steve when we were first married, but I had been a stay-at-home mom for years. The kids were growing up, soon to be out of the nest. The mental abuse I'd been living with had escalated to within a breath of becoming physical. I needed Cross Roads the way a drowning woman needs a life preserver.

The fear that Cross Roads wasn't going to save my marriage became a reality one night when Steve cornered me in a tirade. Grabbing my arms, he blocked my every attempt to escape his rant. Twisting and struggling, I broke free, pushed past him, yelled for the kids, who were laying low in their rooms, and we ran for the Suburban, my husband close on our heels. Jeremy placed himself between Steve and me. As soon as I jumped into the driver's seat, Jeremy scrambled in beside me, and we drove off with Steve still screaming in the distance.

Cross Roads wasn't going to save my marriage.

With the nauseating realization that I was starting over yet again, I began the legal process of disentangling our two lives. I had no idea how I could carry on with what I knew God had called me to do. I'd been out of the work force for quite some time, was at an age where few prospects for meaningful employment were available, and was facing the reality of leaving the marriage with minimal resources.

For my entire life, I'd heard calls to faith, countless calls to rely on God. *Where God guides He provides.* Was it true or not? If not, then I'd wasted a lot of time in church. It was time to decide what I really believed. It was time, as my dad used to say, to fish or cut bait.

In God's time, and not my own, everything is possible.

CHAPTER 5

Gone Fishing

My dad once told me, "Hilda, as long as you're not with a man, you do really well." He recognized the pattern my life seemed to follow, relinquishing control, and then taking control, only to relinquish control again to the next man I loved and trusted. What Dad didn't realize was that he was the one who set the pattern.

With my first husband, I had to assume the full responsibility for my pregnancy. My second husband, Bob, like so many others during the 1970s' skyrocketing interest rates and the 1980s' oil and gas bust, had temporarily lost his direction along with our business. When we lost everything, he took it personally, but he also couldn't stand letting me take charge, and in the end, that's what I do. After Bob walked out, I got by just fine raising Jennifer and our two children by myself, but it was a lonely disconnected feeling. Shortly thereafter, Steve came along, and part of what I loved about Steve was his ability to manage his life. His business was established, he had a nice home: he represented the security, support and social acceptance that many single moms crave.

Like my dad, Steve controlled every aspect of our household, and, following my usual pattern, I went along and went along and went along, until I couldn't.

Finding the property for our retreat marked the moment I began to let go and finally give God control of my life. But the more excited I became about the project, the more Steve dismissed my ideas and tried to organize things his way.

I saw our retreat project as a potential lifeboat for both of us. If Steve had climbed aboard and let God take the wheel, our future might have been different. He saw the retreat as my escape hatch, and the more he tried to slam it down, the harder I had to push to stay on the course I was certain God had set.

Surviving a third divorce is easier said than done. The kids and I went to live with my cousin and her husband for about a month. They were sweet and generous taking us in. I didn't want to overstay our welcome, but qualifying for an apartment, with no job and no money, is tough. There was tremendous pressure from Steve for reconciliation, but each time I wavered my children begged me to stand firm. Steve agreed to pay the rent for the first couple of months. During that time, we completed the property negotiations, putting it in both our names even though we were separated.

God had put me on a path, and I intended to stay on that path. Even as I prayed that creating the retreat project together would heal our marriage, I knew deep down that it wouldn't. And even as Steve and I signed the loan papers to buy the property, I knew we were headed for divorce. That was a devious thing to do, and I struggled with pangs of guilt until I realized that I was forced to take that tack because he had proven during our ten-year marriage that I could not trust him to be fair, especially if he knew there was no hope of reconciliation. I also knew there was no way I could qualify for a loan once Steve and I were divorced, and since we'd put no money down, it wouldn't cost him a penny. God would provide a way to pay for the property, but first I needed that loan.

As soon as I filed for divorce, Steve cut off my credit cards, access to our savings accounts and our investments. He stopped paying rent on the apartment. With a full scholarship at SMU, Jeremy would be off to college in the fall, but Nina and I, once again, needed a place to live.

I was truly at a crossroad: either stay in the apartment and look for a regular day job in Houston or go to Chriesman and trust that God would provide the means to build the retreat.

Prayerfully Focused

Anyone who has ever experienced a touch from God, a push in a certain direction, knows that going back is unimaginable. As my son made preparations to embark on his new academic life, I focused on relocating to Chriesman, never expecting it to be as difficult as it turned out to be. Life in a small town is supposed to be simple and idyllic, right?

Jennifer and Scott were eager to join us but reluctant to resign their jobs until Jennifer obtained a teaching position in the area. She interviewed for positions with several school districts, which required frequent treks from Dallas, a 250-mile roundtrip. Since she would be the only person bringing in a salary, finding a job was critical.

Anticipating finances to be extremely tight, we decided to rent a house large enough for all four of us. We quickly learned that locating a rent house in Chriesman, or even in its nearby and much larger neighbor, Caldwell, proved a daunting task. Because of the scarcity of rental properties, owners could bypass realtors and attract renters by word of mouth. Most good properties were snapped up before they hit the classifieds. We had no local connections, which severely limited our ability to conduct a worthwhile search.

Meanwhile, my divorce stretched out interminably. For ten years of marriage I was asking for very little: half our savings and the property in Chriesman, along with the note, which would be my responsibility to pay. But no matter what terms my lawyer presented, Steve refused to sign. Through that long, hot summer, I stayed prayerfully focused on the objective before me.

Roughing It

Jeremy wrapped up his senior year with the appropriate amount of pomp, circumstance and proms. Nina was out for the summer, as well, so weekends found us packed and headed for Chriesman to continue our explorations. Jennifer and Scott met us at a campsite we set up at the only accessible spot on the entire property.

We knew that making use of existing clearings, if there were any, would minimize the expense of time, energy and money necessary to prepare building sites. The old aerial photo we obtained showed two large clearings connected by a narrow road. We needed to know if the area had been reclaimed by nature or if any of it remained usable. So on a hot July weekend, we decided to go find out once and for all.

The aerial photo also revealed a mystery road running diagonally across the property, overgrown now but visible. Some said it once had been an easement for an illegal pipeline, while others speculated that trucks had used it to take seismic readings during the oil boom days. Maybe it had been a logging road. No one we spoke to claimed to have any actual knowledge of it. We didn't much care. We just knew that if we could find it, the road would provide our only portal into the interior.

That weekend my brother, Dale, and his twelve-year-old son, J, drove out to the property to meet us.

"The only clearing we've been able to find" I told Dale, "is in the far back corner of the land."

"And it's a slow bone-jarring ride," Scott added.

The barely accessible, deeply rutted clay road ran along the west side of the acreage to a small clearing. To say it was hot understates the weather by about twenty degrees. Texas summers are always hot. But in a Texas thicket, surrounded on all sides by vegetation, shrubs and vines that grab at your clothing and scratch at your face, the heat comes at you like a steamroller, sucking the breath right out of your lungs.

The no-see-ums, buzzed around our heads, flew up our noses and into our ears and eyes. Scott and Dale faced a challenge setting up the tents, because the stakes wouldn't hold in sand. Jeremy, with far less hassle, helped me hang my hammock between two oak trees, while the girls searched forever to find rocks for the campfire ring. One hundred feet off the ground, J insanely swayed his tree top perch as he watched the campsite materialize.

Sweaty and grubby by evening, we took a quick trip to town to wash up at the Texas Burger, and then returned to the campsite. Seven city folks snugged up to the fire that hot night listening nervously to howling coyotes in the surrounding woods. Tired but excited, we relished the exploration planned for the next day.

The cool morning air dissipated rapidly as the thermometer streaked upward toward a new record. We cooked breakfast over a little barbecue pit. Then we set out walking through the high grass down the hill, with compasses, machetes, bird-bill clippers, bandanas, and water bottles in hand, the heat already sapping our energy. The road dead-ended at a bank of small cedars. Undaunted, we punched through the branches to find a shallow gully. We were delighted to see the road pick up again on the far side.

When the road did eventually end, we could hear occasional traffic just beyond a dense stand of yaupon. But trekking across the entire property had revealed no sign of the two clearings. We continued hacking through tangled vines and matted yaupon limbs in pursuit of the elusive sites for the remainder of our afternoon, until, mystified, we returned to camp. The unsuccessful effort combined with the searing heat made our long trudge uphill seem endless. Gathered once more around the campfire, too weary to muster much excitement, we silently watched sausages sizzle.

"According to the photo," Jennifer said, shaking her head in bewilderment, "that clearing should've been there."

"I know it's there," Dale said emphatically. "And we *are* gonna find it." He and his son were thoroughly enjoying this adventure.

Early the next morning we broke up into groups of three, each group choosing a different area to search. Instead of dropping breadcrumbs to find our way home, we unrolled lines of neon orange surveyor tape behind us as we pushed farther off the beaten path. At midday, with the sun relentlessly bearing down on us, we called off the fruitless hunt and headed back to camp. Our weekend adventure had run its course. With long drives ahead of us, it was time to catch our breath over lunch and re-hydrate before breaking camp.

Dale didn't show up for lunch. When we had finished our PB&J sandwiches, still no Dale. We were halfway done with packing when he came jogging into camp.

"Come on ..." he panted excitedly, "... come on ... you've gotta come see!"

Hurrying back down the hill, we found where his neon string trailed off before disappearing into the dense foliage. In we went, following the zigzag orange line. Thorns scraped and scratched as we plowed through a couple of hundred feet of thicket.

We quickened our pace in anticipation, when a faint light became visible through the underbrush. A slight draft stirred the stagnant air. Moving excitedly toward the glimmer ahead, we stepped one by one into blinding sunlight. A collective gasp went up. We stared in awe as Dale, with outstretched arms, spun round and round.

"Look!" he yelled. "This is it!"

Waves rippled through waist-high grass that carpeted an enormous circular clearing. Patches of brilliant color flashed as wildflowers danced in the breeze. Wading in, oblivious to the possibility of snakes in the grass, we explored around the edges and located the lost road that led to the second clearing.

With daylight fading there was no time to explore farther up the trail. A long hike back to camp still lay before us, as well the trip back to our respective cities. Whipping out our compass, we quickly determined the direction of the county road, since that would dictate the general direction for a driveway. We noted the position of the sun, where it would rise and set, and where visitors would look first when they came up the drive to Cross Roads.

It was all and more than we'd prayed it would be. We laughed, hugged, and offered up prayers of thanksgiving. The gorgeous meadow encompassed enough acreage for several large buildings.

At the north end of the clearing we could see a rise facing the direction of the county road like a natural God-given platform. The morning sun would illuminate that area. Trees would shade it from the afternoon heat. It was the perfect spot for our first building, a chapel.

Jeremy Derr, Nina Derr and Ginger at our first campsite

Summer Trailblazers

The kids and I settled quickly into a routine during those summer months, spending our weekends at our modest campsite, cooking breakfast on the barbecue pit or eating cold cereal and pastries we'd brought from town. By lunchtime we needed a break from the searing heat and grime as much as from the work. The blissfully air-conditioned Texas Burger fifteen minutes away in Caldwell became our oasis. We'd hit the restrooms, and clean up a little, then eat lunch, drink a gallon of iced tea, and go wearily, but happily, back to work.

Nina was so funny, because she would not pee in the woods. *Would not.* Even after I bought her a bucket with a toilet seat on it, she'd wait until someone could stop working and drive her into town. She's not a rustic individual. But she was a trooper in every other way, working without complaint right alongside us.

On occasion, relatives or friends joined us, finding our great adventure intriguing. Don and Faye Cook, who were building the house across the road, became our first new friends in Chriesman. Despite all the worries weighing on us, we spent that summer in high spirits. Still, the clock was ticking and time was running out.

By the middle of August, Jennifer had not gotten a job offer and was facing pressure to renew her contract with the Garland school district. Scott was understandably hesitant to give notice at his job. My divorce dragged on, and no house had materialized anywhere in Burleson County. Defeat was not an option, but serious disillusionment set in.

Then one night as Nina and I were watching television in our Houston apartment, the phone rang.

"Hilda," said a man's voice, when I answered. "It's Don."

Don? For a moment, I couldn't place the name. It's funny how we can know someone in one context yet feel baffled for a moment when encountering them elsewhere.

"You know we're staying at this duplex in Chriesman until the house is finished," Don continued.

And then I placed him. It was our neighbor across the road from the retreat.

"There's a rent house next door to us," he said, "and guess what. The tenants skipped out last night. No notice, just moved out."

"You mean it's available?"

"If you act fast."

Immediately, I called the owner.

"The house is not furnished," he warned, after we talked for a moment. "You can move in right away, but there's one important condition."

When I hung up, Nina was watching me. I lowered the volume on the television and told her about the house. Although excited about the retreat, Nina wasn't at all happy about leaving her friends behind.

Finally, I said, "The owner asks that we take particularly good care of an antique he has stored in the den. An antique baby grand piano."

Nina's expression went from disbelief to joy, and I watched her previous reservations regarding the move morph into excited anticipation. She had wanted a piano since she was tall enough for her little fingers to bang on the keys of the ancient upright at the preschool.

The next morning we hurried to Caldwell to seal the deal with a handshake, trusting the rest of the pieces to fall into place in God's time. I registered Nina in her new school, as Jeremy was packing up for college life in Dallas.

Jennifer, resigned to renewing her teaching contract in Garland, checked her school mailbox one more time. Among her messages was this note: *Bryan ISD. Please call.*

God's time had meshed with ours as our last prayer was answered. Jennifer had landed the coveted job.

JENNIFER JENNINGS: *We Should Have Died*

For me, the camp was all about the kids. There were incredibly long waiting lists for camps in Texas, and small groups cannot afford a fulltime youth director who knows how to create good study programs, so the kids don't get much spiritual benefit. Often, in these smaller churches, parents take charge of the youth group, and parents rarely have the same teaching abilities as program directors.

So our angle for Cross Roads was to provide programming and to open it to smaller youth groups. That's where I came in.

If a church needed help planning a program, all they had to do was supply the kids and tell us what they were studying. They might be studying friendship or a certain Bible verse, or want a program designed around stewardship. I developed the games, scheduled the day, or the weekend, and facilitated it. When the group arrived, all the adults had to do was help with discipline.

The kids responded well to our programming. Nothing was ever a hundred percent perfect. Occasionally things went wrong, but when they did, it seemed like God was taking a hand. All in all, our retreats worked out. The groups came back, so I guess it was successful.

But at first we were surprised and a little horrified by the lack of support from the community. We expected to be welcomed. We thought people would be excited about what we were doing, and we found the exact opposite. Because our time frame was close to the David Koresh tragedy in Waco, we were considered "the cult moving into Chriesman."

And that was hard. So many other doors had opened for us. Every step had been telling us, Come on in. *Then we got to Chriesman and felt a completely different sentiment. We don't* want you here. Who are you people? You crazy Methodists need to go away.

A lot of what we did in the beginning felt like PR work. Just getting the truth out there, letting people know we were normal, that we had this calling to do a good thing. We tried to get the community involved, but the community didn't want anything to do with us.

Building the camp was physically and emotionally challenging. We did a lot of the work on our own, three steps forward, two steps back. We've all got scars and calluses. One thing after another went wrong, but just when you thought, "I'm done, I can't do this anymore," God would show us a rainbow, another little victory. Look. Here it is. Keep going. Mom, Scott, Nina, and I should weigh 100 pounds each based on the physical labor we did.

But I think doing the work ourselves helped the whole "cult on the hill" thing to go away. People saw us out there working, and they'd stop and ask questions. Working the land gave us validity. We weren't just this group of people from Houston paying locals to do the hard work. We were willing to get our share of calluses and poison ivy.

Another big victory was finally getting our own home. The movers were supposed to come back and help Scott level it, but they didn't. So he had to go under the house with a jack, raise the house up and level it. So I'm lying on the floor with a level while my husband is jacking up our new home on sandy soil.

I'm thinking, "We're all going to die. We finally got a house out here, and this is it. The house is going to fall on Scott, and he's going to die."

Miraculously, he did level the house, and he didn't die. The four of us lived in that tiny house for most of my first pregnancy.

In a dwelling that small, everyone has to give and take, and none of us was good at giving and taking. I think that's why God put us in that house together. We had to learn to adjust to each other's needs, and you'll never find four people better than us for not adjusting. We all had our own ways.

It's funny the things that people wouldn't give on. My thing was, we had to have dinner at six o'clock. Mom and Scott would go off to work, I'd be at home, and I wanted everyone sitting down to dinner at six o'clock.

"We get home at five-forty-five," my mom said one day, when she was frustrated with me. "You want dinner at six, we're not ready, and you get mad."

It was stupid, but each of us was hardheaded in a different way, and we had to learn about giving and taking. When you have one bathroom and four adults, there's a lot of giving and taking. There were a lot of bittersweet moments along with the many small victories. And moments that are funny now, but not so funny at the time, like Mom on the roof thinking she was going to die.

She decided she was going to patch the roof on her own. She climbed up a ladder one Saturday morning, carried the shingles onto the roof, but as soon as she got up there, she was scared to death. She had climbed up early because it grew very hot on that roof during the day. Scott and I had slept late. I finally woke up, and kind of moseyed outside, and there's Mom on top of the roof, just laid out flat, frozen.

All this time she'd been yelling and screaming, throwing stuff on the ground, trying to wake up my sister, who was inside the house, still asleep. Mom saw me and started yelling again.

"Get me down from here! I'm dying up here!" She's on the hot roof at about eleven in the morning. She has no water, and she's frozen, too scared to climb down.

There's no doubt we should have died out there about seventeen times. Those were tough years.

Eventually, we met a lot of good people. We all became involved in the church, but when I went to church, I just wanted to hear the pastor. I didn't want to talk about the camp. Mom, Scott and Nina did that part.

My mom and I and Scott were at odds so much of the time about the camp and what we needed to be doing. Like I said, we're three hardheaded people who all have different ideas. I developed almost a resentment toward the camp and the meetings.

"Just bring me the kids and I'll take care of them," I said. That's the part I wanted to do.

"We're all in this together," Mom argued.

I didn't want that. I didn't feel as good from the camp as from the campers. Mom was differently focused, which worked out well, actually. But it took us a long time to be able to say, "This is your gift, and this is mine, and you can't make me do yours, and you sure can't do mine, so we need to keep our gifts and use them as best we can. And that's okay."

I think most of my spiritual growth and development came from teaching, from seeing how the kids reacted, hearing the innocence and truth in the incredible statements they'd come up with. I would develop this whole program on a subject, and in the middle of it one of the kids would say something so completely not what I was trying to get at but so completely what I should have been trying to get at. It would shake me for a moment, then I'd write it down to remember next time. A lot of self-realization came from the kids, from their experiences and their innocent ideas.

For the elementary or junior high age, we played a game called I Spy Jesus in You. At the beginning of the retreat we set it up by telling the kids, "All weekend long, when you see someone doing something that reminds you of what God would do, what God would say, or how God would treat a person, remember it. You don't have to do anything else but remember it."

Later, we closed the weekend out by asking them to share what they'd noticed. The things they came up with that made them think of Jesus were incredible.

"I thought of Jesus when I saw a flower." And then they'd tell you why, and as you walk around the camp in years to come, you'd see that flower and it would remind you of the person and what they said and the meaning the kids took away from it that day.

Those were the times when I had the most spiritual development. I learned so much from them. It was impossible not to.

There were many times when we didn't know how we were going to pay bills, and on top of everything else that's a stressor. Nina being in high school in a small town, having to figure out how to fit into that community was tough. Mom going through a divorce at the same time she was trying to build a camp was tough. Scott and I were going through our own marriage problems at the time. So we had this whole emotional side element going on. It was almost volatile at times.

But I think we all believed enough in the camp that we were able to, in working the camp, work through some of the other problems. Mom was completely committed to what we were doing.

"This is where I'm supposed to be," she'd say. "This is what I'm supposed to be doing. This is my goal, and I'm not going to take my eyes from it."

That's what pulled it all through, and that's what kept us together as a family. When you see a person you love believe in something that much, and especially when it's your mom, you've got to give it everything you have. Sometimes what we had was not much, but we'd give it.

I have so many good memories. Mostly they revolve around my family. My grandparents came out to visit. My grandfather was very quiet. He didn't say much. We walked down to the outdoor worship area together that day. We'd just put the cross up, and we took him down there to see it, and I don't know if he said anything at all, but he looked really proud. My mom will totally not agree with that, but he was proud of her. I think he couldn't let himself acknowledge that he was proud, because it was so different from how he was raised, his definition of success being the corporate world, and this wasn't necessarily his definition of success. But he did believe in a strong work ethic, and seeing the work she'd put into the camp made him proud.

My grandmother was just silly. And my mom will back me up on this. I had a different relationship with my grandmother than anybody else had. I understood her, and she didn't irritate me like she irritated everyone else. She came out on some of the work days with her twin sister, Sonia, and she'd put branches in the back of the car and would just walk around being silly with her sister. It was as if she lost forty years when she came out there. Big smile on her face. Just happy. She'd sit in the swing underneath the tree and visit with Sonia. Sometimes I'd sit there, too. There was this huge Muscatine grape vine overhead, and every time we'd swing the grapes would rain on our heads. We thought that was funny.

My grandmother was proud of my mom. I got to spend a lot of time with her right before she died. She told me she knew my mom would build the camp because, "Once your mom puts her head to something, she's not going to turn back."

All in all, the best part of my experience with the camp was the family time. We started little traditions, like picking berries on berry weekend, that's still something we do. And having my mom that close, especially when the kids were born, that was great.

This is not just the story of a family who went out to start a camp. It's a story about God finding a family to go out and start a camp and then to tell the story.

When all you have left is God you have all
you need to start again. – A. Copeland

CHAPTER 6

Movin' On

On a beautiful, hot August day, pulling a rented U-Haul trailer behind my Suburban, I set out for our new home. Nina, sixteen, had thrown on her favorite Christian t-shirt and shorts, before tucking a bag full of snacks under her arm and piling into the passenger seat. Now, her blue eyes flashed with excitement as she sat beside me nervously twirling her blonde locks and babbling like a brook.

"Mom, what do you think it's going to be like living so far away from everything?"

"I don't know. I guess we'll have to find out together."

"What about the school? Do you think they'll have a snack bar? How many kids will I have in my class?"

"I've never lived in a small town. I just know God's going to be there for us, and I know it's going to be good." We filled that Suburban with so much joy, relief, and excitement I'm surprised it didn't *float* all the way to Chriesman.

The following weekend Jennifer and Scott planned to pack up their worldly goods and hit the highway traveling south from Dallas. Scott would drop Jennifer in Chriesman then return to fulfill his responsibilities at the magazine. Jeremy would jump in the little black GMC pickup and head west from Livingston, Texas where was working a summer job as a camp counselor. Each of us harbored personal reasons for needing a fresh start, were headed for a country lifestyle none of us could have imagined a year earlier.

The Houston population in 1996 numbered over three million, with Dallas trailing close behind. Chriesman had a population of 70. That's not a typo, seven zero, *seventy* people in the entire town. I'd bump into that many people in a Houston shopping mall.

Caldwell, just down the road from Chriesman, boasted nearly 4,000 individuals. Forty miles away lay the flourishing metropolis of Bryan/College Station, which numbered about 120,000 people. Talk about culture shock. We'd lived all our lives in big cities. But I think every one of us was ready for a simpler lifestyle.

Houston, except for its multistoried office buildings and elevated expressways, is flat. Northwest of Houston the terrain begins to gently rise and fall. As we approached Chriesman, in the early evening, clouds were building at the end of the road, the kind of clouds that sit low to the ground in big puffy violet mounds. They looked like beautiful, distant mountains. Not a skyscraper in sight.

Although it would be years before I stopped glancing over my shoulder expecting trouble from Steve, that was the moment my nerves started settling down. There in the distance, like a mountain to be climbed, awaited our grand adventure. For better or worse, we were going for it, no turning back. It was like the nail-biting pause before the highest loop on a rollercoaster, scary but also exhilarating.

*Nina Derr, Scott Jennings, Jennifer Jennings, Jeremy
Derr and Hilda Hellums at home in Chriesman*

At Home in Chriesman

The U-Haul held my few possessions. Steve had claimed the house
and furniture, so I'd taken only the pieces I owned prior to our
marriage, mostly a few small tables left to me by my grandmother.
Nina had her daybed. Before leaving Houston we'd stopped at
an antique auction barn and found a simple oak bed and night
stand for me, which we bought at a thirty-percent discount
after mentioning we were moving to Burleson County to start a
Christian youth retreat. Later, we stopped in Brenham and bought
a mattress set for the bed. We counted on Jennifer and Scott to
supply the remainder of our furnishings, which meant living with
the bare necessities for a while.

Jennifer arrived early in the day. Nina and I drove in late that
evening. Tossing our sleeping bags in a back room, we bedded
down for the night. Scott wouldn't arrive until the next weekend,
and Jeremy, stressed to the max about school, the divorce, and

breaking up with his high school sweetheart, was coming, too, to help unload. All my kids were acting every bit as excited as I felt about moving here.

The next Saturday, Jeremy arrived first. A few hours later Scott drove up in a U-Haul truck. Running out to greet him, Jennifer, Nina and I froze in our tracks.

Scott was backing the truck across the septic tank toward the back door when the truck clipped the anchor cable on a fifty-foot TV antenna. Leaning and swaying, the antenna headed for a fall.

We ran out and grabbed the cable. Pulling and pushing, we were able to reattach it to the ground bolt and avoid the catastrophe. But what an upsetting way to start our new life!

While we trudged back and forth, unloading the U-Haul, the couple next door strolled over with their son, Joe, and introduced themselves.

Andy and Rita Kay Isaacs, a few years younger than I was at the time, were about as different from each other as sugar and spice. Rita Kay was tall, slender, her outfit perfectly put together, every hair beautifully in place, and her makeup impeccable.

"We just moved down here from Granbury, Texas," Rita Kay told us.

"Is that near Dallas?" I hadn't actually heard of the town, but when people mentioned moving "down" from anywhere, it was usually the Dallas area.

Andy nodded. "Thirty miles from Fort Worth."

In jeans, work boots, and a "gimme" cap, Andy looked exactly like a cowhand who'd just come in from the barn. He made me feel a little less scruffy in my jeans and flip-flops.

"You've heard of Dinosaur Valley State Park?" Rita Kay said. "That's in Granbury."

"We were tired of being squeezed in with traffic and noise," Andy added.

Joe was a typical teenage boy, about Nina's age, and they went off to talk by themselves.

"What brought you to Chriesman?" I asked Rita Kay. Unlike her husband, she looked like a woman who'd fit best with city life.

"Our dream brought us," Rita Kay said. "We found the perfect piece of land."

"A hundred-and-sixty acres just over the county line," Andy added.

"We're starting a Christian youth retreat there," Rita Kay said.

Hearing their plan took my breath and gave me goose bumps. What were the odds: our two families coming from opposite directions to the same place at the same time, buying the same size tract of land, and with the same agenda? I knew immediately that God had a hand in our coming together, but I had no idea what to make of it.

Hunkered Down

Now that the first part of my vision had become reality, one day followed another, all of them filled with more work than I'd expected. I was in a siege mentality, too busy to stick my head up. Some days I truly believed that the yaupon was growing back behind me as fast as I could chop it down. At night I hunkered down in my office trying to figure out our new life and how I was going to pay the bills.

Steve eventually signed the divorce settlement, but the check failed to materialize in my mailbox no matter how often I called my attorney. I lived in a state of constant tension waiting for the phone to ring, the mail to arrive. When the day came that we were forced to spend our last two nickels, I borrowed $5,000 from my parents, using for collateral the diamond bracelet that had belonged to my great-grandmother.

Jennifer started her new job. Nina started school. We hacked yaupon and greenbrier on weekends and watched the weeks march by as our resources dwindled again. Ironically, I hadn't made time to find a new church home or any kind of Christian connection.

About that time one of my next-door neighbors, Brenda Gaskins, began hounding me about meeting a friend of hers. Brenda was a cheerful, friendly young mother of three with blonde shoulder length hair. Her friend lived "just on the other side of Chriesman," where Brenda pastured her horse.

Once again I was too busy trying to figure out things on my own to get involved with people in the community. I kept putting Brenda off, and putting her off, and putting her off, but she was relentless. One day she dropped by and found me, as usual, sitting in the dark, my face lit by the computer screen, books and papers scattered on every surface.

"I'm going to check on my horse. Come get in the truck and go with me. You need to meet my friend."

Not today. Wearing my usual cutoffs and t-shirt, my hair air-dried and unruly, I just didn't need this right now. "Brenda - "

"No excuses. You need to do this. Come on."

"Brenda, look at me. "

"Nobody cares what you look like. You look fine. You look like you can use a break."

Saying "no" obviously didn't work with her. Resigned to the fact that the only way to get her off of my back was to go and get it over with, I said, not very graciously, "Okay. Fine."

"Won't take long," she added, smiling. "The work will be here when you get back."

"I said okay, so let's just go!"

Just the other side of Chriesman turned out to be a rambling twenty-minute trip down a winding country road to a washboard gravel side road that ended abruptly as we bumped nosily across a cattle guard onto a sandy, riveted, half-mile drive up a hill. All I could do was grumble inwardly, *Where the heck is she taking me? I can't believe I let Brenda talk me into this.*

No matter where you've been or how broken you are, God still
wants to use you. But you've got to let Him.

CHAPTER 7

Angel on Wheels

Our tires squished over sand, crunched over patches of caliche, and mercifully came to a stop. A half dozen dogs erupted into barking at our approach. Their raucous alert sent a solitary figure on a riding lawnmower scurrying off behind the main house.

"Cindy," Brenda yelled, "this is my new neighbor I've been telling you about."

A small woman with piercing eyes popped around the corner of the house buttoning her shirt as she walked. We'd obviously interrupted her sunbathing as well as her mowing. Cindy VanDeventer, a slight woman, about eight years my junior with pert, elfin features framed by shoulder length brown hair, looked me over.

"Let's have a glass of lemonade," she said, "and we'll talk."

I don't have time for chit-chat, I'm losing daylight standing here. But saying "no" probably wouldn't get us home any faster.

"Sure," I said. I was learning that country life moves at a much slower pace.

While Brenda checked on her horse, Cindy and I sat down at a weathered picnic table. The cold lemonade tasted really good, and Cindy's warmhearted but no nonsense attitude soon wiped away my desire to rush back home.

"Tell me about this retreat Brenda says you're building," Cindy coaxed, after we'd chatted for a few minutes.

I explained that God had put the idea into my head and on my heart during a retreat the kids and I attended in South Texas. I rattled on about searching for the property, convincing Steve, divorcing Steve, and the mounting anxiety I felt as each day passed.

"The mission that seemed so God-sent and practical only weeks ago now seems impossible to complete," I said. "The divorce settlement, if the check ever arrives, will be only enough for living expenses. Our business loan *has* to go through, because we desperately need money to start building the retreat."

"What you need is to connect with a new Christian support system," Cindy assured me. "Come to church this Sunday. There are some people I want you to meet. Then we'll work on your next step."

This was my introduction to Cindy VanDeventer. Only later did I realize I'd met my guardian angel.

The Walk to Emmaus

Cindy was a fixer and a helper, and I was in dire need of both. Cindy simply lit up at the challenge of introducing me to the local Christian community. Her fixer-helper skills jumped into overdrive. First she invited us to her church, where we were welcomed with open arms, then, she invited me to her women's Sunday school class, where I was embraced as a sister. She also taught a Bible study in her home called "Experiencing God," which gave me valuable tools for discerning His will in my life.

"What you really need, though," Cindy had told me that day under the oak tree, "is to go on the next Emmaus Women's Walk."

"That sounds time consuming." I'd heard of The Walk To Emmaus but had no idea what it was or what people did there. I'd been on retreats, however, great retreats. In fact, I was building a retreat. Right now my time would be better spent getting the business loan so we could survive until our project was completed. But I didn't say no. "Maybe later."

"Hilda, you need this, and the timing is perfect. It only happens here twice a year. Lucky for us, there's one planned for September."

Next month? "I don't know if I can do it right now, Cindy."

"Yes, you can. You've been working too hard on your own. You need God with you. You need to be fully in His presence again. And Emmaus is all about spiritual renewal."

She was beginning to sound like my eight-year-old Jennifer begging me to go to church. "What do people do at this retreat?"

"I can't tell you about it, Hilda. You just need to go."

"But you said it's a walk. A walk to where? What happens?"

"I can't tell you that. You have to go and experience it for yourself."

"Sounds very secretive."

"Not really, it's just that talking about it won't give you what you need. Every experience is different. You have to do it for yourself."

What about cost? What about ...?

I soon learned that it does no good to argue with your guardian angel. As it turned out, Scott went on the walk two weeks before I did.

The Walk to Emmaus takes place in two parts: one for men, one for women. The name derives from the story in Luke 24:13-35, and each part is a three-day experience that provides an opportunity afterwards to connect weekly in a small group. The entire community comes together monthly to share their experiences and celebrate their renewal and their reconnection with God.

Scott arrived just in time to kiss Jennifer, unpack all their furniture, and barely get settled before leaving for his weekend Walk. I knew that when he returned I could squeeze all the details out of him.

Let me tell you about Scott. He is the epitome of tall, dark, and handsome: a little over six feet tall, athletically trim, with dark brown hair, brown eyes, and a quirky sense of humor. He is a kind, and talented individual, who tends to be stern at times and has high expectations of everybody, including himself. He's a hard worker, always going the extra mile.

So when I told him that, in addition to getting as much clearing done as possible before winter and helping me finalize the business plan, he also needed to go on the Walk to Emmaus, Scott didn't argue. The men at church signed him up to go. But when he got back, and I asked him about his experience, Scott was less than forthcoming.

"It was a great weekend. You're going to enjoy it."

"So tell me what it's all about. What did you do?"

"I can't tell you. Just go and do it and be open to whatever happens."

And so I did. And he was right, there's no way to explain the enormous impact Emmaus had on my life. Yes, it's a retreat for spiritual renewal, but it's so much more than that. Before you renew you have to get rid of your baggage, through meditation, prayer, fellowship and sharing. For the first time in my life, and

I was forty-six years old, I realized that I wasn't alone anymore. I wasn't the only woman who felt certain she'd messed her life up beyond repair. I wasn't the only woman struggling to overcome the effects of a difficult childhood and my own bad choices. I wasn't the only woman who felt that, in a world of normal people, she was the odd duck, the problem child, the one who didn't belong. I realized that it was okay, God still wanted to use me.

In that community of loving acceptance, I realized that I'd come to Chriesman feeling broken and unworthy. Who am I to be starting a retreat for kids when I'm divorced three times? When I'm less than a perfect mother? When my kids are less than perfect, and if they are perfect, then it was God's hand not mine that guided them? Who am I to be doing this? Nobody's going to take me seriously.

There were sixty women on our Walk, Christians from all over Central Texas, and after listening to some of their stories, I knew that no matter where you've been or how broken you are, God still wants to use you. But you've got to let Him.

The other amazing experience of Emmaus is the enormous community of loving support. You come together as strangers and leave as best friends, with a boundless source of mental, moral, spiritual, physical, and emotional support. There's nothing you wouldn't do for one another.

I'm sure if I hadn't gone on that Walk, I'd have limped along and somehow God would have completed His work with or without me. But Emmaus was an important step in healing, a huge step that would normally take years, compressed into a three-day weekend. The Emmaus community surrounded my tenacious family with supportive Christian people who were almost as excited as we were about our ministry. Some suggested that our Cross Roads retreat could answer their prayer for a perfect location to hold their events. One of the most enthusiastic voices came from Jim Smith, President of the First National Bank in Caldwell. Jim was not only from Houston, but had been the scout leader and mentor for one of my neighborhood friends. We made an immediate connection.

"As soon as your business plan comes together," Jim said, "bring it to me. Funding shouldn't be a problem."

Funding shouldn't be a problem. His words lifted me like wind beneath my wings.

If you ask the wrong question, you are going to get
the wrong answer. – Dr. Gaines S. Dobbins

CHAPTER 8

Not in the Plan

With high hopes of financial support from our local bank, Scott, Jennifer, and I jumped with both feet into creating the business plan. Scott completed his marketing survey, documenting beyond a doubt that there was a need to be filled. My friend from Houston came through on his offer to help with the blueprints and cost estimates. He designed a superbly functional multipurpose structure, with a kitchen, dining hall, conference room, and dorms downstairs, plus housing for us upstairs.

Jennifer continued putting together programs the retreat would offer. Since we intended our ministry to accommodate many different denominations, our programs wouldn't address theological issues, but would focus instead on teambuilding, working in harmony, being the body of Christ, supporting one another; themes and subject matter all Christians agree upon.

We operated in high gear during those fall months, fired up by Jim Smith's enthusiastic endorsement of our project, not to mention his efforts to help us obtain the building funds. During this time, my settlement check from the divorce finally arrived. For our years together, several of which I'd worked with Steve to double his agency's business, I received my fairly new Chevy Suburban, 160 acres of beautiful "good for nothing" land with a mortgage far exceeding my net worth, and $45,000.

A Stinging Revelation

Despite our limited resources, I was completely against holding a job. I viewed going back to work as a potential distraction to the mission God had placed on me to fulfill. While the settlement didn't provide a huge nest egg, and came at a time when we were pinching every penny, it meant we could move forward even before the bank funded our business loan. We wanted to be ready for the spring retreat season.

Scott, too, wanted to stay focused. He's a hard worker and would gladly have taken a job, using his evenings and weekends to handle what needed to be done at the camp, but that would mean hiring someone to help with jobs that required a man's strength. Jennifer and I were strong, but we had our limits, and paying contractors for the work would rapidly deplete our scant bank account. So Scott and I continued spending our daytime hours working the land and our evenings working the plan.

During this time, we became well acquainted with our new friends, Andy and Rita Kay, who were moving forward with their own plans for a camp in Milam County. And while our missions were seemingly the same, we had some lively debates about just how God expected us to go about accomplishing His will. Rita had a successful home-based career, which enabled Andy to devote more time to their new ministry. Our different approaches didn't interfere with our willingness to help each other. We cleared land together, at their place and ours, celebrated birthdays together, and spent many a night playing "reverse hide and go seek" in our conjoined yards.

One person would hide, the rest would seek, and when someone found the person hiding they would hide with them. The last person not hiding was the loser. Our landlord's ancient Mimosa, a tree native to Texas, frequently concealed up to five of us in it's branches.

Anyway, country life is different, slower, more intimate, and we enjoyed those occasions with our new friends. Andy proved to be an invaluable mentor for Scott during a rocky period in his life. He and Jennifer, I learned, were facing some serious challenges in their fledgling marriage. They viewed our project as an opportunity for healing and recommitting to each other.

Thanksgiving came and went. Jennifer and Scott visited his folks while I spent the day with family in Houston. Everyone returned home from the holiday eager to continue investigating the tangled interior of our domain.

An avid reader of action adventures and historical sagas, I was always up for exploring new areas of our land. One day we encountered a thicket as dense as a jungle and a swamp worthy of an Indiana Jones movie. Jennifer and I decided to cross it using an old Indian trick I'd read about.

We cut down saplings and placed them upright in front of the underbrush. Then we walked down the trunks like a balance beam, and the saplings flattened the thick vegetation before us. A carpet of pressed foliage lay just above the mucky water. It actually worked!

On another excursion, Scott took the lead, followed by Jennifer and I. Scott was swinging his machete, slashing a path ahead, while we hacked away at the brush on either side. With a sickening *thud* Scott's blade hit a hollow branch.

"Watch out!" he yelled.

Behind him, Jennifer and I couldn't see the problem. Our first clue came as a sting, followed by more stings. A swarm of bees came flying out of the branch.

Turning tail, we ran for our lives, terrified that we were being chased by Africanized bees. Jen was in the lead now, I was second, and Scott brought up the rear, all of us swatting our way through the swarm as we tried to avoid the stumps and fallen branches of brush we'd chopped down earlier.

"Ow!" I tripped and rolled.

Scott halted to avoid stumbling over me. I got up, lurched a few steps and fell again.

"Hilda, come on," he yelled, trying to help me up while waving the bees away.

"No, Scott, go on!" With my heart racing, my lungs constricted, I gasped dramatically, "If they get me they get me."

Scott grabbed the back of my belt and hoisted me like a satchel. With my rear in the air, my head bobbing dangerously close to the ground, and my feet flopping around, he ran for the cab of the trusty white farm truck we'd bought. Jennifer held the door while he tossed me inside and jumped in behind me.

It's funny now, thinking how I must have looked, but it was heart-stopping back then. My children still tease me about it, and we laugh so hard tears stream down our faces.

Not long after that grand adventure, we got news about our loan. Jim Smith was no longer our loan officer, because the bank had changed hands just after we submitted our application. Jim had moved to a different location, and the new bank that took over had much more stringent underwriting rules. With little thought, it seemed, they had rejected our loan.

I'd never realized that God's blessings might
wear plaid jackets and earflaps.

CHAPTER 9

Down and Out

After pulling ourselves out of the stupor of that first rejection, we naively took the loan application we'd spent so many weeks laboring over to another bank.

"Sorry, we can't fund this project."

And another.

"Sorry, you simply don't have enough collateral."

And another. "Sorry."

Looking back, I wonder where I found the nerve to keep hammering on doors. Can you imagine banks refusing to loan a quarter of a million dollars to a divorcee with no collateral, no job, and no prospects, just a 160 acres to her name, and with a loan against that? I laugh about it now, but I must have been crazy to think they'd even consider it.

Rapidly, our world was falling apart. We'd been laboring so hard for so long, and so many people were behind us now, that we felt like we'd been sucker-punched. After the last rejection, we were too upset to discuss it for several days. We sat around like zombies, too tired and dejected to even cry. Once again, our dream was over before we'd scarcely gotten started.

Out of Options

We continued praying, or rather ranting, to God. Our friends commiserated. They seemed almost as miserable about our loss as we were.

But life had to go on. We had located the two clearings, so using a portion of our meager funds; I hired a dozer operator to clear the drive we'd loosely identified as the best entry from the county road. With more than a dozen tall oaks to knock down, it was much too large a project for machetes or axes.

Scott had a knack for ferreting out information and finding people. He'd go into Woodson's, a builder supply store in Caldwell, hang out with the good ol' boys who'd lived on farms and ranches all their lives, and return with the sort of knowledge you can't find in library books. Never in a hurry, he'd read all the cards people posted on the bulletin board. Whatever we needed, he'd just start talking to people and eventually he'd come home knowing exactly what we had to do.

That's how he found Buddy, a dozer operator whose conservative fees fit our miniscule budget.

"You want a driveway cleared, is that it?" Buddy asked, when he came to check out the job.

"From the road, it would have to go about a quarter mile to a clearing, where we plan to build," I told him.

"Got a lot of land here. Word around town is you're making some kind of religious camp."

"A youth retreat, yes."

"Religious camp."

I could see visions of the recent debacle in Waco with the Branch Davidians in his eyes. "Nondenominational weekend retreat," I assured him. "Nobody stays here long term, except for my family. Churches will bring their youth on weekends."

"What sort of religions?"

Buddy objected, it turned out, to particular denominations, and he wasn't certain he could do the work we wanted unless we assured him those churches would be excluded. Of course, we couldn't agree to that, and for a while it seemed to be a deal breaker.

"Our doors have to be open to anyone God sends our way," I explained. "We're creating a place where God's presence can be felt and heard. It's not up to us to decide who comes."

Eventually, I must have said the right words to assuage Buddy's concerns. Using the aerial view again to find the boundaries of our property, we searched for a path of least resistance, which means the fewest large trees. This part took a while, because aerial photos don't come with boundary lines marked, and we didn't want any mistakes.

Once we had our bearings, we used surveyor tape again, tied it to a bush and started walking. Buddy came along later and dozed everything on the path. Watching that dozer work, doing so effortlessly what we couldn't have done in weeks with our hand tools, convinced me we needed to buy a tractor at some point in the future.

When it was finished, we discovered it was about five feet from the property line. God must have been smiling that day: by the skin of our teeth, we got it right.

Enter Carol and the Boys

In the process of clearing the driveway, Buddy knocked down a number of big trees and unceremoniously shoved them to the sides of the new access road. This not only blessed us with an endless supply of firewood, but also with hours upon hours of drudgery cutting them up, splitting the wood into firewood and hauling it away.

One evening Nina got home from school and told us that a boy she'd met on the bus had asked if his family could cut up a few tree trunks for the their wood-burning stove. You bet they could! I was overjoyed at the prospect of having the downed trees removed for free. Time passed, though, and no one came, so most days after work we whittled at the task, chain-sawing what we could and dragging off a few chunks at a time. The request from the young man on Nina's school bus was forgotten.

Then one chilly fall afternoon I drove onto the property and was shocked to see three hefty lumberjacks in heavy plaid coats, work boots, gloves, and caps with upturned earflaps, hoisting chainsaws. Spying them, I felt curious at first, then apprehensive. Then my territorialism kicked in, and I moved to investigate these folks who were cutting up my trees.

Billy, the boy from the bus, had brought his brother, Clint, and his mother, Carol. I soon learned that the three of them lived a mile up the road on five acres Carol had bought a few years earlier. Their house had been a hunters' cabin, and the family was in the process of remodeling it. They needed firewood because their sole source of heat was one wood-burning stove.

As Carol and I talked, I shared the story of our coming to Chriesman and our plans. She thanked me for the wood, then offered to help in any way she and the boys could.

Until then, I'd never realized that God's blessings might wear plaid jackets and earflaps. But after that day, Carol and her boys became a part of our family and have blessed us in more ways than I can count.

Many are the plans in a man's heart, but it is the
Lord's purpose that prevails. - Proverbs 19:21

CHAPTER 10

God's Rogues

No one can appreciate a road until you've had to travel on overgrown trails for months. Our new driveway was all sand and bumps and treacherous soft spots, even after we toiled for backbreaking hours making it safe to drive a car over. Nevertheless, seeing that road clear was a dearly needed shot of adrenaline.

With that adrenalin boost, a new direction for funding slowly began taking shape in our minds. If we couldn't borrow money to build the camp, we'd have to become a nonprofit organization, with tax-exempt status, and solicit donations.

That was never our plan, and the idea didn't set well with me. The prospect of being a nonprofit forced many adjustments in our thinking, but the one that annoyed me most was that a board of directors would have to be appointed, which meant giving up control.

Obviously, God had his own plan, and He wanted Cross Roads to be completely His, not mine.

Rogues

Reluctantly, we began the daunting process of obtaining an IRS Tax Exempt Status. I knew that not everybody who applies gets the exemption, so we were apprehensive going in.

I sent for the forms, and an intimidating packet, at least an inch thick, arrived to further terrify us. I didn't even know which exemption we might qualify for, there were so many, each with a long list of qualifications. I consulted a lawyer for assistance, who said I needed an accountant. The accountant sent me to a different lawyer. I repeated this round robin several times. Bottom line, there was no professional help available to us.

So once again, I checked out books from the library, appreciating for the first time my mother's way of teaching. She'd handed me a cookbook one day, saying, "If you can read, you can cook." God seemed to share her teaching style.

Scott and I decided we'd have to figure it out, one page at a time. Since Cross Roads wasn't a religious organization, we didn't qualify for many of the tax exemptions. We weren't pastors, and we weren't planning to preach. We were not looking for a congregation or any particular set of followers. Most camps or retreat centers, we learned, fall under the umbrella of an established denomination or organization. We didn't have that. We were rogues.

Not having that umbrella caused us to worry about whether we'd be able to do this or not. But we read the parameters and decided that our goal to provide a place for mentoring, teambuilding, socialization and education to churches and other nonprofits would qualify us under section 501(c)3 of the IRS tax code.

The math alone was mindboggling, and as anyone who knows me will tell you, I don't do math. But we calculated our cost and income projections, based on the facilities we planned to build and

Scott's surveys of how far people were willing to drive and what they'd pay. Scott taught me how to use Excel to create a spreadsheet, how to put in the formulas so that the calculations were easier and accurate. I was so proud of myself: I actually did it.

At last, we wrote our mission statement, which was critical. We learned from our books that the best mission statements are short, to keep the organization focused, so we determined that:

Cross Roads would be committed to strengthening & building community by

- *Creating a sacred place where Christ may be encountered and faith renewed.*

- *Cultivating spiritual growth through faith-forming experiences.*

- *Reflecting the light of Christ's unconditional love and acceptance to all.*

- *Providing a refuge for learning, inspiration, and transformation.*

Absurdly, when the thick stack of "official" government forms was completed, signed, and ready to mail, I was scared to send it in. This was our last shot. We still had no money, no hope of a loan, and if we couldn't get tax-exempt status, which was key to our receiving nonprofit funding, it really was over.

I worried that our package wasn't good enough, and was terrified of a rejection from the IRS that would seal our failure and our fate. So in a fit of insecurity, I shoved the application to the back of a drawer.

A Diamond In the Rough

At a time when we all needed our spirits lifted, my wedding rings sold for $2,500. Of the many, many uses I could apply that money toward, the one that brought the biggest smiles to all our faces was buying a tractor.

"Think of all the things we could do faster and easier," Scott coaxed.

"Clearing, mowing, hauling stuff," I agreed. "But where could we buy one on our budget?" I'd seen farm equipment for sale, and even a city girl can tell from a distance that tractors cost a lot more than $2,500.

"An auction." Scott showed me an ad.

Farm Equipment Sale
Sealy, Texas

Sealy was a town about two hours south of us, and for city people, this promised to be another great adventure. When sale day came, we loaded up in the car and drove south to Sealy.

The thing I noticed immediately was how quickly heads turned when we walked by. Nina and I were the only women there.

We walked around the sale lot and looked at the items marked for auction. Before long I spied a gray and red tractor I liked. The fact that it was a Ford 9N model was lost on me, since I knew nothing about tractors. It didn't have a lot of bells and whistles, which I figured was a good thing. It had a "user friendly" look to it.

"Do you think we should bid on it?" I asked Scott.

"Let's watch for a while, see what the others go for."

We watched three of them go, and then our tractor was up. When I started bidding, heads turned again. I know the men were wondering, *What's up with this woman?*

71

The exciting thing about an auction is not only the expectation of getting a bargain but that quiver in your stomach when you think, *What if it's a piece of junk? What if I'm throwing the hard-won cash from selling my wedding rings into a red and gray money pit?* Then you think, *But, what if it's a great a deal?* Then again, you think, *Am I being foolish, what in the world makes me think I know what I'm doing?*

We bought our tractor for $2,500. And we had a lot of fun bidding for it.

Then we had to get it home. Fortunately, a man from Caldwell who regularly attended the auctions and whose business was selling used farm equipment offered to haul our tractor to Cross Roads for fifty dollars.

Once we had the huge tractor unloaded at home, we realized that it was a two-ton diamond in the rough. It ran really well, was easy to operate, and that old red and gray blessing came in handy for just about everything.

A diamond in the rough

Hands in Motion

Meanwhile, Jeremy was struggling with his studies at SMU. A bright student with tremendous aptitude and an impressive IQ, he had fun during his first college semester. In fact, Jeremy had so much fun that he lost focus, lost his scholarships, and came home to us at Christmastime riddled with frustration and disappointment.

The tradition of giving homemade ornaments for Christmas began that year. Jennifer and Scott came up with a cute and clever angel design. The five of us chipped in for the materials. Playing Christmas music and munching on Christmas cookies, we worked for hours until we had crafted angels for all of our friends and family.

Then Jen and Scott drove off to one of his parents' homes for Christmas. That year was my Christmas with Jeremy and Nina, meaning they were not visiting their dad for the holiday. Christmas Eve we squeezed into the kitchen together to prepare our special dinner. As usual, we ate our Christmas dinner on Christmas Eve then exchanged gifts before leaving for the Christmas Eve service at our new church.

Sitting there with two of my children at my side, surrounded by new friends, I felt both blessed and content, no matter what the future might bring. We exited the darkened sanctuary; lit only by handheld candles illuminating loving, smiling faces, and I enjoyed the warm sensation of being safe.

Later, before we turned in for the night, as is my tradition, I read the first chapter of *God Came Near,* by Max Lucado. The kids, being almost grown, did not pop awake at dawn but slept in fairly late. Still, they awoke expecting gifts from Santa and a Christmas brunch. They were not disappointed.

A Sudden Departure and a Confrontation

As the days passed, Jeremy fell into a funk. At first he'd joined wholeheartedly in working on our retreat project, contributing wherever he was needed. He worked at Woodson's, setting up their new computer system. Then one Saturday morning I found a note on his pillow. He was headed for Houston to make his own way. Gone.

In a world before cell phones, I could think of no way to find my son, short of hiring a detective, and in all honesty, what did I have to offer Jeremy if I did find him? Worried sick about where he was going and what he planned to do, I prayed for him and left it in God's hands. Jeremy was more levelheaded and self-sufficient than most eighteen-year-olds, and with God's love, I knew he'd be all right. Still, I felt sick inside that I'd failed Jeremy at this critical time in his life.

Saturdays were big workdays for us, with Jennifer and Nina at home to help. So regardless of wanting to take the day to locate Jeremy and make sure he was indeed okay, I held it together and put on my work clothes.

Yet my mind festered with questions I couldn't answer. If I was truly doing God's will, how could it happen that I would lose my son? What kind of plan would God have for me that didn't include Jeremy's happiness?

Every blow my machete dealt to the hapless yaupon that day was accompanied by a mental cry of self-doubt, anger, and recriminations raging inside me. When my turn on the tractor came, I backed it up as usual and watched as Jennifer attached the chain to a stump.

Our strategy for mastering the yaupon was effective but time consuming. An evil bush, yaupon. When left to its own in the wild, it grows into squatty trees, spreading by its root system and creating an impenetrable wall of brush. First, we'd hack off the tops of these trees. Then taking turns at the wheel, one of us would back the tractor up to the stand of pruned trees, wait for someone to wrap a chain around a stump, then rev up the engine, pop the clutch, and yank the yaupon out of the ground by its roots. We had it down to a science.

As soon as Jennifer attached the chain, I revved that engine, popped the clutch and something gave way inside me. Stomping the accelerator, I sped out and kept going faster and faster, yelling and screaming at God, crying, and asking his forgiveness all at the same time.

That confrontation with my Heavenly Deliverer seemed to go on forever, although it probably lasted only a few minutes, and in the end I knew I had to let go and let God handle Jeremy in His own way. I had to trust God to take care of my boy, because I could not do it.

When I returned to the yaupon patch, completely spent, Jennifer and Scott greeted me with questioning eyes. But they respected my silence.

*Let us not be weary in well doing: for in due season we
shall reap, if we faint not.* - Galatians 6:9

CHAPTER 11

Hard Headed

As the government forms for acquiring our tax exempt status
lingered in the back of a drawer, our depleted funds reached a
critical low. One night Scott and Jennifer broached the possibility
of my going back to work.

"No, I don't think that's a good idea." Working anywhere but
at the camp was not in my plan. "As soon as we're officially a tax-
exempt nonprofit, we'll get the funding we need."

"Where? People don't just send money because it's tax
deductible." Jennifer looked at Scott for support.

"It's going to take time," Scott said. "Meanwhile - "

"Meanwhile, I still have some money to keep us going."

Jennifer showed me our list of "Things to be Done." At the
top of the list was "finish the water line," which meant buying
a quarter mile of PVC pipe. "Build the chapel" came next, along
with a price tag far beyond the remaining funds in my bank
account. That $45,000 was a spit in the bucket compared to what
we needed for cabins, a dining hall, an office, living quarters, not
to mention the note on the property and daily living expenses.

"I could get a job," Scott offered. "I'd still be free on weekends."

"That makes even less sense. You're skills are critical around here, and without your help, I'd get very little accomplished." I knew I was being obstinate, but I was determined that God would make it work. That night I took the application from the drawer and reviewed it.

Sand and Water

Early on we had run a pipe from the main water line about six feet onto our property, and attached a faucet, so water for drinking and washing up wasn't a pressing problem, we only had to drive a quarter mile from the clearing to fill our containers. But brush piles were stacking up all over the property, and to burn them safely we needed water.

Scott rented a trenching machine and dug a trough alongside our driveway to lay the water line. Jennifer and I followed behind, trying to place the twenty-foot lengths of PVC pipe before the sand spilled over and refilled the trench. Each piece had to be fitted to the next and glued.

Needless to say, none of us had ever done this before. When we finally attached the up-line, waited for everything to dry, and turned on the spigot, the puny trickle of sandy water that emerged was like Manna from heaven.

Unfortunately, a puny trickle was the most we could get. Scott went up to Woodson's and asked a couple of his priceless ol' boy contacts what we'd done wrong. Not a thing, they assured him. We just used the wrong size pipe.

At the dinner table that night, we were all noticeably quiet. The entire water line would have to be redone. I knew Jennifer and Scott were brooding over the hard work and money we'd wasted. I knew they were also worrying about our dwindling bank account and my single-minded determination not to get a job. What I didn't know was how to reassure them that God

77

would not have brought us this far only to turn his back when we were down.

To Be Moved

Despite the reality that our paperwork was still languishing in a desk drawer, we kept moving forward as if the tax-exempt status was a done deal. We reevaluated our plan from the perspective of being a nonprofit, and Scott hit on a great idea.

"I've seen ads for 'house to be moved,' and the houses are usually pretty cheap," he said one day. "I'll bet people would donate those buildings if they could take a tax deduction."

Such conversations often took place while Jennifer was at work, Nina at school, and Scott and I were resting after spending a few hours of yanking yaupon out of the ground.

"We'd have to pay someone to move the houses," I said. "What does that cost?"

"Can't be as much as building from scratch."

We began watching the ads, and then we placed our own ad in the area newspapers:

WANTED
Houses to move for a Christian camp.

"I have just what you need." The call came from a Mr. W.P. "Bill" Strube, Jr. He sounded elderly and full of excitement. "I have an entire Christian camp, no longer in use. Several buildings. I need them moved, and they're yours free for the taking."

My help comes from the Lord ... Psalm 121:2

CHAPTER 12

Mr. Strube

An author* and founding member of both International Christian Radio and the Frontier Christian camp in Crockett, Texas, Mr. Strube was now in declining health. He was putting his affairs in order and wanted to clean up some property for his wife.

"The camp started out right there on my land," he told us. "And operated there for many years. Later, they relocated, but the original buildings have remained ever since."

A rush of excitement overtook me, that same surge I'd felt on learning that the Moody Bible Institute had property to sell. "Are the buildings large? Small? Can they be moved?"

"Easily. Several of them, at least." Over the phone, his rich voice sounded as reassuring as the late Walter Cronkite's.

"What do you need from us?" I asked, trying hard to conceal my enthusiasm. God, I decided, must have sent Mr. Strube to give us the boost we needed. With only a few cabins and a dining hall, we could get the camp going, start the income flowing, and Jennifer and Scott would stop urging me to get a job.

"Move 'em out and give me a tax receipt. That's all I need."

Elated, we quickly made plans to meet him in Crocket the following Saturday.

"It's a straight shot on Highway 21," Scott told me. "Less than two hours driving time. Shouldn't be hard to get the buildings moved in."

I put the cost of moving them out of my mind. God had provided the buildings; He would provide a way to get them moved. Spirits were high as all four of us jumped into my Suburban and took off east for Crockett, arriving early at the designated meeting place, a local Burger King.

Mr. Strube, however, was quite late. The ticking clock over the door grated on our already taut nerves. Finally, a spare man in a rumpled suit and starched shirt pushed through the glass door with a woman I took to be his wife. Quietly attentive, Mrs. Strube had graciously accompanied her husband to the meeting.

"Y'all must be pretty important!" Mr. Strube said, obviously flustered. He shared with us the compilation of mishaps that had conspired to keep them from getting there on time. "To top it off, a buzzard flew into our windshield. Have you ever heard such a thing? One of those black devils you see feasting on road kill up and down the highway."

"I've come close to hitting one before," Scott said. "Never had one fly into the window."

"Not a pleasant experience, trust me."

We visited for a while as they regained their composure. Mr. Strube had moved many buildings, and he delighted in explaining the intricacies to us. Eventually, we were off to see the old camp.

Rot

The state of decay was irreversible. Not only were the buildings unusable, they were also unmovable. A pine tree had fallen through the roof of one. Others were rotten from the ground up or had gaping holes in their roofs.

Our hopes, which had been so high, nosedived at the dizzying speed of light.

"Oh, sure, they need a little fixing up," Mr. Strube said. "Y'all shouldn't have any trouble doing that."

"I'm not sure," I stammered. Concealing the depth of our disappointment from the gracious gentlemen and his wife was impossible.

"It'd be a help to us both," he persisted. "Y'all need the buildings to get started, I need the land cleared and a tax receipt. A wonderful opportunity all around."

Scott and Jennifer were dumbstruck. Mr. Strube's precious camp buildings were not an option.

"We haven't actually secured our tax-exempt status," I reminded him.

He chuckled and said four precious words I'll never forget, "Just send it in."

"But I've heard it's not that easy to - "

"Naw, don't be afraid. Just do it. The IRS will mark it up in red ink and tell you what you need to fix. No one gets approved the first time. Y'all make the corrections, send it back in. May take two or three times. Let the IRS be your lawyer, and just don't be afraid."

The very next day I took our application out of the drawer and mailed it in. We'd done our part, now all we could do was wait. The wheels of the Internal Revenue Service turn extremely slow. Once again, however, God had sent an angel to open a door for us, and once again it wasn't the door I expected to open.

Daily Grind

The approval of our 501(c)3 tax status would change everything. I knew that, and I had faith that we were now on the right course. Unfortunately, Jennifer was right when she said, "People don't just send money because it's tax deductable." Fundraising is a process. It takes time. People need to see that the money they donate will be put to good use. And until our tax-exempt status was approved, we couldn't solicit donations.

We desperately needed to begin building, though, as a sign that Cross Roads was alive. With Mr. Strube's camp a complete washout, we continued scouring the local newspapers for other possibilities, while one hard fact kept hitting me in the face: I had to get a job.

The money from my divorce settlement was not going to last much longer if we kept using it for living expenses. With a job, I could earmark some of the remaining funds to buy and move any houses we found that were suitable.

I hated the idea of going back to work. Sad, scared, and forty-seven years old, I'd been out of the workforce a long time. But it wasn't just that. Going back to work was like admitting I'd failed. Spiritually, it was devastating. My wonderful God-given idea was slipping away like sand through a sieve.

*Mr. William B. "Bill" Strube was co-author of *Eat, Drink & Be Prepared (For tomorrow you may live)*.

We were not alone anymore, praise be to God.

CHAPTER 13

Letting Go

Humbling myself to ask for a job? I don't do that well. I suppose it's my entrepreneurial attitude working against me.

Bob and I had owned and operated a successful business for many years before the economic downturn. Then I helped Steve build his business, thinking all along that it was "ours." And in all my sales jobs, I worked on commission only, which means the harder and smarter you work, the more you make. That's the essence of entrepreneurial spirit.

Now I was fully in control for the first time, trusting in my belief that God wanted to use me to fulfill a mission, using my professional abilities to carry out that mission. It's hard to go back from there, hard to retrace those steps toward identity and independence and revert to working for someone. I hadn't had a "boss" in many, many years. My burning interest was in Cross Roads, in running it like a business and making it the success I envisioned God had in mind. Could I put my heart into just earning a paycheck?

In the end, I did what I had to do, but spiritually, it was all too humbling.

State of Grind

When I was married to Steve, my insurance came through his agency. Now, needing a new auto insurance card, I stopped by a local agency to pick one up. Owned by a man and his wife, a wave of déjà vu struck me as soon as I stepped through the office door.

While the man printed up my card, we started chatting, and I told him what I'd done to help build the agency in Houston. He was immediately interested in learning more.

"So, you're no longer with that agency?" he asked.

"Divorced. I live in Chriesman, now, about forty-five minutes from here."

"So, what business are you in now?" Behind his eyes, I saw wheels turning.

I told him about Cross Roads, about Scott and Jennifer, about taking a job until the retreat was built and running on its own income.

"Could you do for us what you did in Houston? Call on realtors, bring in new business from homeowners?"

Just like that I had a job. It was a bittersweet moment.

Daily life became really hard. No more cutoffs and t-shirts for me. Instead, I had to get up early every morning and make myself look presentable for calling on realtors. I gave it everything I had, and they seemed happy with my contribution to their business, but Bryan wasn't Houston and a lot had changed in the industry over the years.

The forty-five minute commute meant that I rarely had any daylight left at the end of my day. The only time I could spend improving the property was on weekends.

One day I asked God, "What are you thinking? You gave me this thing to do, and it's not working out. I can't build and run a camp, maintain a paying job, and raise a teenager all at the same time. I know you won't give anybody more than they can handle, but I'm there, God. You're about to push me too far."

We had that conversation, and it didn't change anything. Yet I felt better afterward.

Hand in Hand

An entrepreneur has the option of running a business solo or hiring a board of directors, maintaining sole ownership or going public. As head of a nonprofit organization, I would no longer hold such options. A board of directors was necessary, and their collective votes would shape the direction Cross Roads would take.

We started with three directors, me, Jennifer and Scott. I wasn't ready to trust anyone else, yet. In advisory positions, it was easy to find willing and able members. Nina became our energetic Youth Advisor.

The Cross Roads mission fired people up and made them want to participate. With the guidance, encouragement and hard work of our friends and advisors, we were ready to strike out on our new path.

Meanwhile, Scott scouted around every day for houses, gathered information about moving houses, and continued clearing space for the cabins, conference room, and dining hall we needed. He also researched inexpensive multi-purpose buildings.

The word that Cross Roads would operate as a nonprofit began spreading. An industrious new friend, Mary Stevens; volunteered to help us finance the camp. Five-foot-six, and a blue eyed blonde, Mary has the sweetest, softest heart of anyone I've ever met. A genuine, loving, caring person, she's a divorcee, with one son. I met her through Emmaus, and she became my best friend even before she began soliciting donations from all over central Texas.

A cotton candy booth at the Caldwell Kolache Festival contributed to our building fund. Another new friend generously provided a dozer service to clear a space where the buildings would eventually be situated.

A few cash donations trickled in, but not nearly enough to build the significant structures needed for a proper camp. Our independence from denominational ties opened the door for donors who might not be inclined to give to a particular denomination. However, we suffered financially from not having the safety net that a denominational affiliation would provide.

We needed an additional show of faith in our project to engender confidence from the community, so I took a deep breath and pitched in a chunk of my remaining cash. I earmarked the seed money to install utilities, to purchase building materials and cedar picnic tables.

In addition to an open-air pavilion that could be used for dining and other group activities, we would use the materials to create teambuilding stations. Jennifer undertook the challenge of identifying low-element stations that could be easily installed by volunteers and would present the least liability to the camp. Jeremy returned specifically to design a Blindfold Maze that could be built using cedar posts. Last but not least, we planned to install a pen for a petting zoo, which Jennifer thought would be a wonderful draw for elementary age campers.

By pointing us in this direction, a nonprofit, tax-exempt facility, little by little God was prying my fingers off the control stick. I now believed that if we purchased the building materials and put the word out, our new friends and neighbors would rally to help with the construction we so direly needed. And so we did:

Cross Roads
Breaking ground with a good old-fashioned barn raising.

The barn raising

The Barn Raising

During the week before the event, it rained almost daily, effectively preventing us from any significant preparation. The building materials arrived, ready for troops of volunteers to officially kick off the construction, but the picnic tables had not been delivered.

The morning of the big event dawned behind a cold, drizzling gray sky. Our new driveway, which ran uphill to the clearing, had been topped with red clay. Now the persistent moisture turned it into a nasty slippery slope. As carloads of excited volunteers, some from as far away as Houston, drove enthusiastically up the hill, the driveway held together, but the ruts deepened with each arriving vehicle. Eventually, it degraded into a slop of shoe-stealing muck.

The opportunity to witness the "happening" drew several of my family members to Cross Roads that day. My mother, her twin sister, Sonia, my brother, Dale, and my youngest sister Sandra, all turned out to help. Curiosity probably had a lot to do with it, but I think they were also cautiously optimistic that they might actually be a part of something big. Both five-foot-five, fair, with auburn hair that framed knockout blue eyes, my mom and Sonia pitched in with gusto, helping Carol with the food and taking lots of pictures. As the day progressed, I saw the glimmerings of pride and excitement dance in their eyes as they joined in our belief that Cross Roads would someday become a reality.

Mid morning we sighted a truck at the bottom of the hill slipping and sliding, wheels spinning, as it attempted to pull a heavy trailer loaded with picnic tables up the drive. Half way to the top, it surrendered to the intractable mud. Within minutes, a swarm of volunteers encircled the truck and bravely mud-wrestled the tables the rest of the way up.

Work details formed and dispersed to begin construction. Amazingly, women out numbered the men, and dripping wet, they wielded hammers, nail guns, saws, and all manner of tools as if they'd been construction workers all their lives.

So much had changed since we first arrived in Chriesman labeled as the local "cult." I cornered my amazing family, Jennifer, Scott, Nina and Jeremy, and we clung to each other in a group hug.

We were not alone anymore, praise be to God.

Cross Roads became the calm in my storm when my son, Joey, was at the Boys Ranch in Waco. Where did I go every time I'd leave the Ranch from taking Joey back? Cross Roads. That's where I knew I needed to be. I had to feel God, and that's where I felt Him.

The first time I heard about Cross Roads was at Emmaus. Hilda gave a talk about the youth retreat she was building, and I thought wow! When she described her vision and how it came about, I was inspired. Immediately I wanted to be involved in it. I wanted to do whatever I could to help kids, too. My heart at that time was with the youth, because of Joey.

On the Saturday of the barn raising, I came out to work, and brought Joey, and we helped build the Wall at the obstacle course. The next day was a work day, too, but Joey and I were the only ones who showed up.

Hilda never gave up. No matter what problem arose, she just kept going. She'd say, "Okay, we've got this little road block here, now let's see how we can go around it."

She'd get down sometimes, and I knew she was wondering if she'd made a mistake. Then I'd get mad and say, "If God told you to do it, it's gonna work no matter what."

We were good for each other. I needed Cross Roads and they needed me. God put us in each other's paths for those times we needed to be there for each other. I truly don't know what I would have done without that connection.

When I look back, there are lots of good memories. Like building the little shed. It was hard being out there, nailing those boards. We worked in the rain with a nail gun. I remember we couldn't get the nails to go in on one side, so we went to the outside and made 'em work backwards.

I told her I'd help with financing Cross Roads, and I came up with a garage sale idea. For months people brought stuff to donate. We had to rent a storage unit to hold it all. We spent the night before the sale at Baker Exploration, where I worked. Pat, my boss, was generous about letting us hold the garage sale in the company parking lot. If he hadn't been so flexible, I never could have done so much with Cross Roads. Any other person, when I asked for weekends off, would've said, "You want off again? No." But Pat always said, "Yeah, that's okay."

Anyway, we slept on air mattresses that night, getting up every few minutes to make sure our garage sale items weren't walking out of the parking lot. We raised $1,200, but I don't think we advertised it well enough. We had a ton of stuff left over.

One of my favorite programs at Cross Roads, which we can't provide anymore, was the Cross Walk. Jennifer created it. She has such a talent and such a bright, happy smile. She'd say, "Let's do this, it's going to be wonderful," and even in the worst circumstances, it was.

Cross Roads touches so many people in so many different ways, and I know Hilda has heard this from a lot of us, but Cross Roads is a good, good thing.

There 's never been a doubt in my mind that God is at Cross Roads. At certain places there, I feel really, really close to God, and I'm not the only one who has said this: "When you are at Cross Roads you know God is present."

You can feel Him. That feeling is tenable, tangible. It's there. God is there.

It wasn't about the buildings.

CHAPTER 14

Milano House and the Rainbow

We had just booked our first "retreaters" when the phone rang.

"Hilda?" Our landlord sounded cheerful. "I've got some good news and some not so good news. I just got married!"

That must be the good news. He'd been divorced, so I wondered if the "lucky" lady was someone I knew from the area.

"Congratulations. I look forward to meeting her."

"Here's the thing," he said. "The house you're staying in, we're gonna want to live there."

"Oh. I suppose we'll have to find another place to live when our lease is up in August." This was May.

"Yeah, but that's the thing. If you remember, nobody actually signed a lease. But don't worry about it, I can give you a full thirty days to find a new house."

So much for handshakes, not only did we need to find another rental in a town where renters only gave up a house when they died or won the lottery, we also had to move and prepare for our first group of retreaters all at once.

Considering our options, we realized that we didn't want to look for rental property. We knew from experience how long that might take, and besides, renting was a waste of money. We really needed to be living on our property. Otherwise, during a retreat, we'd drive ourselves nuts running back and forth.

We decided against manufactured housing, not certain we could even qualify for a loan on one if we wanted to. Scott's research had proved there were houses available to be moved. We just needed to find one in our limited price range. Scott began checking the want ads again.

Ten miles up the road, in Milano, he found a small farmhouse. On farms, it's not uncommon to see a big new house with an old house sitting right alongside it. When families outgrow the original structure, they build their dream home next door and either rent out the old one, use it for storage, or tear it down. This farmer wanted the original structure off his property.

Scott drove us there to see it, and it didn't look like much, but we were desperate. The clock was ticking.

"It's tiny," I muttered, knowing we didn't have time to keep searching. "But the hardwood floors are nice."

"I love the kitchen cabinets," Jennifer said. "They're beautiful."

She was right, they were natural cedar, carefully crafted, and included a bin for storing flour, as was often found in old farmhouses. They were also short, perfect for Jennifer, who was five-foot-three. Scott, at over six-feet tall, would have to do dishes on his knees.

The owner agreed to sell it for our magic number, $2,500. Tiny or not, that was a bargain. His only qualification was that we had to move it and leave the site clean. Simple enough, or so we thought.

Dumb 'n' Dumber

We hired the only house movers we could find who were available on such short notice. *Available*, that should have been a red flag.

I was at work on the afternoon the big move was scheduled. The second red flag popped up when Jennifer and Scott met the movers in Milano. From Scott's research, and Mr. Strube's instructions that day at the Burger King in Crockett, Scott knew that house movers use a fine-bladed reciprocating saw to cut a house in half then load the two halves on wheels.

Dumb 'n' Dumber showed up with no saw at all. They borrowed Scott's chainsaw, promptly broke it and then asked him to fix it. Jennifer and Scott watched apprehensively as "Dumb," the tall one, fired up the saw and began cutting the house in half crosswise.

Scott had measured the tight spots on the road. He frantically tried to convince them to cut the building along the ridge row at the roof peak, so that it would travel down the road without a problem.

Jennifer, distraught, chose that moment to tell Scott she was pregnant with their first child. Unfortunately, his response did not reflect his joy at the news. Instead, his expression tightened into a grimace as his fear of failure to provide a decent home for his wife and, now, a new baby, suddenly impacted him.

Dumb n' Dumber slid two iron rails under the first half of the house, jacked it up, attached the wheels and slowly began to drive forward. As Jennifer and Scott watched them pull the two halves apart, their hearts sank. In the cross sections, they could see gashed sheetrock, splintered wood floors, and jagged roof tin.

Dumb led the way as the pilot car, Dumber pulled out with his load, and Jennifer brought up the rear. When they made it through the field where the house had sat and onto the road without getting stuck, Scott began to breathe again.

"It's not what I expected," he muttered to himself, "but I can fix it. It won't be as pretty, but I can fix it."

Suddenly, he realized that they had not put slides on the roof to guide utility wires over the house. He communicated that failure to the two "movers," and clambered alongside Dumber (the skinny one) up onto the roof to lift the wires over the house by hand. In disbelief, Scott watched him nail boards, to act as slides, through the metal roof, causing further damage. Worse yet, he left a nail protruding, which caught the next wire they passed, ripping it off the utility pole of a nearby house.

The drive down Highway 36 went fairly smoothly. Then they turned onto the narrow and winding, tree-lined road we called our own, and the full impact hit of cutting the house crosswise. Instead of the slim profile that cutting along the ridge row at the roof peak would have provided, the widest part of the house presented itself flat to every tree and branch along the road.

From behind the lumbering procession of pilot car and house, Jennifer watched in horror as they bounced over the railroad tracks and the floor beam began to split. Then they came to the tightest spot on the road, right in front of our landlord's precious rental house.

The county had given us permission to cut any branches hanging over the road. In fact, every landowner along the road had given us permission to trim any trees we needed to trim, except our landlord, who was inordinately fond of the humongous mimosa tree we had hidden in while playing Reverse Hide and Seek. As they approached it, Scott climbed on the roof again and tried to move the Mimosa's limbs out of the way. He even removed a small limb.

But Dumb, the driver, said he was taking too long.

"Stand up with a chainsaw and cut the limbs while I drive," he suggested.

That was too much for Scott. He climbed down, Dumber took his place, and they drove and cut for about fifteen feet, where they reached the biggest limb on the Mimosa. Dumber tried to duck while Dumb barreled on through. They struck the limb, breaking the eve of the house and tearing up the roof.

By the end of the second exhausting day, the two halves of the house sat dejectedly side by side in the clearing at the top of our long driveway. The roofs were demolished, the floors buckled, and the walls leaned dangerously in random directions.

We stared in disbelief at the shattered remnants of our house.

"Okay, that's it for today," Dumber said, loading up to leave. "We're out of here."

"See you on Saturday," Dumb added.

That was two days away. Never mind that rain was on the horizon, with the two shattered halves of our house open to the elements. Never mind that we expected our first group of campers on Saturday and had no time to deal with protecting our investment from further ruin. Dumb 'n' Dumber were taking the weekend off.

Too numb to cry, we erupted in righteous indignation and outright anger. What were we supposed to do now? Holding hands in front of our expensive piles of rubble, we prayed asking God just what He was thinking and for guidance.

The Milano house

Comes the Rain

It was too late to cancel the day trip for the fifteen excited third-graders God was sending to us. Somehow, we had to make this work.

All we'd built so far was the open-air pavilion, the obstacle course, and a petting zoo, which the kids were really excited about. We'd been nuts enough to put an ad in the paper actually soliciting animals that needed a good home in the country. The outpouring of animals was both heartening and overwhelming. We had two pet goats that loved to climb on cars, a potbelly pig that was used to sleeping with its previous owner, a gaggle of ducks that fouled their "kiddie" wading pool daily, a former FFA Blue Ribbon sheep that knocked you flat at feeding time, and Jack, who was called a "Jesus" donkey because of the black stripes that ran across his withers and down his back.

For the retreat, we were scheduled to facilitate a teambuilding program, a service project and, of course, feed our visitors. On

Friday, Jennifer and I at our separate day jobs watched black clouds roll in and time drag out interminably until quitting time. Once again we were racing the clock. After work, I hurried to buy hot dogs, hamburgers, charcoal, and the materials we needed for the service project. Jennifer was at home ignoring the ringing phone and the landlord on the caller I.D. She struggled to focus on completing an agenda and gathering supplies for the program.

Meanwhile, Scott was also watching the weather with increasing apprehension as the radar lit up with flashes of an approaching thunderstorm while our farmhouse was still sitting in halves. A heavy rain would melt the sheetrock and warp the floors and cabinets, destroying what was left of our adventurous new living quarters.

He rounded up Nina and Brenda Gaskins' strapping fifteen-year-old son, Chris. Since introducing me to Cindy VanDeventer, Brenda and her family had become close friends. Scott and Chris piled into our rickety white Dodge work truck we called the "Ghost" and headed for town, where he bought rolls of plastic to cover the exposed sides of the house.

Eyeing the approaching storm and the task at hand, he told Chris, "If I get struck by lightning or fall off the roof, and if I'm not dead, grab a board and either finish me off or knock me out."

Nina was to go for help, since she could drive. It was sprinkling as Scott anxiously climbed up the ladder and onto the tin roof.

None of them had ever seen lightning strike so close, each bolt hitting the ground with a terrifying fury. As Scott secured the last of the plastic, the heavens let loose with a torrential Texas downpour.

Spent, soaked to the skin, and exhausted, he drove the kids home and helped finish preparations for the next day's arrivals.

Fun, Games and Obstacles

The van with fifteen third graders and their handlers pulled up to the wreckage that was our house and stopped. Kids jumped out and began scattering.

"Sticks, sticks!" the boys yelled, running to the edge of the woods, where they snatched up broken branches to use for frog hunting.

The counselors, dutifully concerned about the hazardous materials in the middle of the camp, listened incredulously as we told them what had happened to bestow on us the plastic-encased carcass of our soon-to-be home. After calming their fears, we introduced ourselves and welcomed them to Cross Roads. We cautioned the kids to stay away from the old house, with its protruding nails, sharp edges, and splinters.

Not an auspicious start for Cross Roads, but I couldn't help recalling my first youth retreat experience, arriving late at night after a five-hour drive to find the camp dark and our hosts less than communicative. At least this group had only been on the road for forty-five minutes from College Station.

Jennifer kicked off the program with a heartfelt prayer, asking for safety and for the Holy Spirit's presence. To break the ice and get to know the kids' names, she passed around a basket of random objects: a pen, a paperclip, an eraser, a golf tee, and other miscellaneous *stuff*. Everyone picked an item. Then they were asked to tell the group their name and how the object might relate to them or to their Christian life. One girl picked up a battery and said she had a lot of energy. A boy chose a rubber band and said he was flexible. The exercise proved enlightening, as well as fun, and I swelled with pride for my daughter's natural aptitude for teaching and working with kids.

Afterward, Jennifer divided the group into teams and pointed them toward the Obstacle Course. The kids ran ahead of us.

Unfortunately, the house was directly in their path, presenting an irresistible opportunity for mischief. By the time we caught up with them, kids were hanging all over the wreckage. Frantically, we lifted down one wriggling child after another and sent them scurrying.

Once everyone had assembled at the Obstacle Course, Jennifer began explaining the objective.

"Look, a frog!" a boy yelled.

It leapt into a deep hole and, to our horror, the boy went in head first after it. He was up to his waist when Scott grabbed him by the belt loops and yanked him out. Grateful that a skunk or a snake hadn't greeted him, I was tempted to ban elementary-age kids from ever coming back.

"Your teams will be timed," Jennifer said, continuing her instructions as if the interruption had never happened. "The team to complete all ten obstacles in the shortest amount of time will be the winner."

Yips and squeals and hoots sounded as they practiced being winners.

"*However,*" Jennifer said, loud enough to get their attention, "after you start, everyone on the team has to finish one station before moving on to the next. Are you ready?"

"Yeah!" they all shouted at once.

"On your mark ... get set ... go!"

The first team hit the Overs 'n' Unders and streaked to the Stump Jump, then came to a screeching halt. The stumps were too far apart for them to step, leap, or jump from one to the other without touching the ground. After a few minutes of hurling themselves, and failing miserably, they figured out that they could help each other. It was heartwarming to watch the stronger ones assist the weaker ones, the tall one help the shorter ones, and a swarm of little ones helping the bigger ones.

From there they ran to the Rope Swing, the Burma Bridge, the Swinging Log, the Tire Run, the Blindfold Maze. When they ran up to the final element, the Wall, one girl hung back. She was terrified of heights.

"We'll help you," Jennifer assured the girl. "Don't be afraid. You can do it."

After much coaxing, the girl finally went for it. With her teammates hoisting her from behind, she scrambled to the top and leaned over.

Jennifer grabbed her hand. "Keep going, you can do it."

The girl froze.

Jennifer kept saying, "Come on, come on, you can make it!"

Timidly, the girl said, "I know I can, but you'll have to let go first."

Jennifer let go, and the child slipped the rest of the way over the wall. When her feet hit the ground, she was beaming with a newfound sense of pride, accomplishment, and community.

The second team won. They almost always do. They use what they learn by watching the first team.

At the end of the day, we gathered the teams to play, "I Spy Jesus In You." The first to speak was a boy. He looked at the girl who was afraid of heights.

"I spied Jesus in you when you were on top of the wall," he said. "You were afraid, but just like Jesus takes care of us, you trusted us to take care of you."

Jennifer, Scott, Nina and I, making eye contact, smiled with the realization that something profound had just happened, and it had nothing to do with buildings. Cross Roads was destined to be a success, not because of any quarter-million-dollar facilities, but because God was working in and through everyone who came here to touch lives.

Back to Reality

After our new friends left, waving, shouting, and vowing to return soon, we took just enough time to shake off the incredible gratification of completing our first retreat before turning our attention to the house. Scott had to virtually threaten Dumb 'n' Dumber with bodily harm to make them help us cobble the structure back together. Otherwise, they had no interest in finishing what they deemed now to be an impossible job for hostile clients.

The days ahead grew constantly more frantic, as we spent every afternoon following our day jobs trying to reconstruct the house and make it habitable. Almost every evening my landlord called threatening to send the authorities to evict us if we didn't move out. We worked our tails off to comply with our landlord's demands.

Once the house was sealed against the elements, we spent the next few weeks making the interior livable. The 900-square-foot interior was divided cottage-like into four equal quadrants, a kitchen, a living room, and two bedrooms, with a small covered back porch and a tiny bathroom tacked onto the back. Scott spent Saturdays at the local coffee spot and hardware stores gleaning how to, how not to, and other general wisdom from the local men.

Library "How to" books saved the day once again, as we studied electrical wiring and plumbing. Scott enlisted Brady Rockett, a youth from church, to help rebuild our cottage. We could not have done it without him. We rewired the electrical sockets and replaced fixtures. We repaired sheetrock, patched walls, textured, and painted. We enclosed the back porch with plywood for Nina's bedroom. The original walls between the rooms were also made of plywood, held in place by straps attached to the ceiling. The house had no air conditioning, and occasionally a pet goat would pop its head through the floorboards to say, "Hi."

On moving day, rain was ironically in the forecast once more. Nervously watching the sky, we scurried back and forth on the three miles of county road, from rent house to farmhouse, carrying everything we owned in the back of our open pickup. The clouds grew darker and more menacing with each trip. Pushing the last load safely into the house, we breathed a long overdue sigh of relief.

The first drops of rain splashed the tin roof as Carol, our dear friend, who had helped us through the rebuilding and the moving, drove away. A moment later, we heard a car horn honking loudly and repeatedly. When we ran outside, Carol was waving her arms crazily and pointing up to the top of the house.

Running into the yard, we looked back over the house to find the most vibrant rainbow I've even seen. Maybe it was exhaustion, maybe it was relief that such a traumatic time had finally ended, or maybe it was joy at this exquisite sign of God's love, the sign that He keeps His promises to the faithful. Whatever the stimulus, seeing that incredible rainbow hovering over our cobbled-together cottage, we all dissolved in tears.

It wasn't about the buildings, that rainbow seemed to be reminding us. It was about the people who would come to Cross Roads and who would leave there touched by God's hand.

"I have been to good camps, and I have been to great camps. I now have been to a Godly camp. May God bless you and your staff for a memorable time of worship."

- CBCC, Cross Bend Christian Church

SCOTT JENNINGS: *I Was Young and Didn't Know Any Better*

Yaupon and sugar sand, those are the first two words that come to mind when you say "Cross Roads." After that it is a flood of emotions and memories. Once Jennifer and I decided we wanted to help with the camp, we went at it just as passionately as Hilda did. The camp is so intertwined in my memories during that portion of my life that it is hard to discern what was Cross Roads and what was personal. Looking back, I can see God's hand in putting people together and guiding them to work on His project.

I was raised to go to church. Faith was quietly important to my immediate family. They attended formal services occasionally. My grandmothers also encouraged me in my faith by sending me to church camps every summer. The thought of starting a camp like the ones I fondly remembered attending gave me the warm fuzzies. I felt like it was a good thing. I felt moved to do it.

The more Jennifer and I talked about it, the more excited we got. It seemed to fit everything we wanted.

Creeping up the corporate ladder in Dallas had quickly lost its appeal. I also found Dallas overwhelming at times. My college days were spent in College Station and San Marcos, where I discovered that I liked the pace of life in a smaller town. I always enjoyed having projects to do. I grew up doing projects with my dad and grandfathers, asking questions and absorbing as much as I could. Jennifer and I had worked out at my parents' farm, enjoying the property while helping them clear land and build the house. We often spent the trips back talking about getting a place of our own one day, so the idea of having land really appealed to me.

When I was a child, my grandfather always had a calf in his herd that was "mine." I dreamed of raising cattle one day. So when the opportunity arose to move to Chriesman and help start Cross Roads, I jumped on it.

Chuckling inside, I saw that Hilda had already posted a map on the bulletin board and had traced a ninety-mile radius around Houston. She was looking for a location. Wow! She's gonna get after this, *I thought*, it's gonna happen.

I didn't fully realize just how small Chriesman was or the challenges that came with it. It was a big change from being raised in the city by parents with small-town roots to actually living in a small town. With that change came a lot of mental pressure, mostly from myself. When I told my family of the plan to move and start a Christian camp in the sticks, they were supportive, but I could hear the apprehension in their voices.

After we had spent some time in Chriesman, I put even more pressure on myself. When you are married, that tension spills over to your spouse. I felt like I had to behave as well as a preacher, work harder than any farmer and make my family, especially Jennifer, just as proud of me as they could be.

I stayed at home while Jennifer went off to earn our living. She never said a word about that, and frankly I never thought about it until one of the men in town made a comment about how hard it must be to work land "that won't be making money any time soon knowing your wife is the one bringing home the bacon." That comment made me want to work even harder.

Also, it was physically tough at Cross Roads. Working on my own much of the time, I had to come up with some extremely creative strategies using pulleys, ropes, wedges, and all manner of things. Naturally inquisitive, I had no problem seeking help, even if it was only advice, from folks all over town. I would work through a project in my mind and then run it by someone in town or call a family member to ask them what they thought.

At first there was nothing I couldn't do, because I was young and didn't know any better. Over the years my confidence and ability grew to the point that there wasn't much of anything I couldn't do or figure out. Most days I looked up from work to find Hilda or Jennifer, mostly Jennifer, wondering why I was still working in the dark. I had no concept of time and never wore a watch. Jennifer finally gave me a pocket watch, and that helped, if I remembered to look at it.

I never felt that I got enough done. I had a list of things to do for the property, for the camp, for our house, for Hilda's house and for our sanity. Each list was broken down into priorities, then by affordability and finally ranked by what was funded and what wasn't.

In my mind, nothing was ever nice enough or good enough. I was my own toughest critic and unrelenting taskmaster. I knew I could do better. Living with my mother-in-law, brother-in-law and sister-in-law was stressful, especially since Jennifer and I had gone through a difficult time in our relationship and were trying to mend fences. So, with the tension of raising teenagers on one side of the house, and the tension on our side of the house, I was surprised the house didn't just catch on fire.

The little white house we bought and moved onto the property reminded me of my grandparents' beach house in Florida or the little house my dad grew up in. It was small, simple. It was ours. And there were a lot of times when there was a lot of love in that house, and there were times when there wasn't. Mostly I remember the happy times.

The first night we spent in our house, it was HOT. Poor Jennifer hated being hot, but at least we did not have to worry about the nagging landlord anymore. Emotionally, our life was a rollercoaster. We had gone from a big rent house to a small house of our own that we still shared. Me, three women and all of our worldly possessions stuffed into less than a thousand square feet of barely livable space - this created an interesting dynamic. My desire to make the camp work grew stronger and stronger, partly to provide the home my growing family deserved.

Moving to Chriesman to build the camp was the beginning of my spiritual awakening. The moment I walked into the First United Methodist Church in Caldwell I felt comfortable. I felt like I was home at last. The process of going to church, Christian fellowship, and the Walk to Emmaus helped me build my relationship with the Lord and a supportive community of faith. Working at the camp provided limitless opportunity for prayer time. I talked to Him the whole time I was working. I got to where I felt as comfortable talking to Him as I did fussing at Him. Although, fussing at Him does no good, really, other than maybe make Him smile. I love God and I love what He had us doing out there. I was ecstatic, bordering on manic. When everything was going right and everyone was just as tickled as punch, I was happy beyond belief. I got down when things weren't going exactly the way I wanted, but somebody in the family, or in our network of friends, or even in a group we were hosting always managed to point out God's greater plan.

Cross Roads: the name meant a lot to me then and still does. When we came up with the name I knew it had special meaning for me, and now that I look back I see that the choice I made at each crossroad in my life was critical. Regardless of all the turmoil and stress in our personal lives we still worked together to build the camp that God wanted. Every group that came there wore us out physically, but reading the comment cards renewed our spirits.

> "I am so thankful that I am able to stay with my friends and become closer to God on this magnificent weekend. The amazing help it gives me in life is indescribable."
>
> – Allen

But my God shall supply all your need according to His riches in glory by Christ Jesus. -Philippians 4:19

CHAPTER 15

Houses and Cabins and Bunks, Ah-ha!

Although it wasn't about the buildings anymore, there was still a critical need for two cabins and enough bunks to accommodate the people we expected God to send our way.

Two of our new church friends generously and anonymously donated toward our first cabin in memory of their father's. And after the successful barn raising, my dad viewed my "retreat folly" with new eyes and had donated toward a second cabin. God truly does work in mysterious ways. Years later, I'm still amazed at the significance of my father's generosity.

We looked through camp furniture catalogues and found sturdy wooden bunk beds at $500 a set. The costs were too staggering to think about. That was a hurdle looming in our future.

More pressing was the massive work needing to be done on our tiny farmhouse before it would approach anything resembling comfortable. The tensions among the four of us living together in 900 square feet were growing daily, right along with Jennifer's pregnancy. I know that people survive in worse housing situations, but not without hardship. I didn't want to damage our family relationships, so call me crazy, but on top of everything else, I wanted to find a separate house for Nina and myself.

Meanwhile, there were not enough hours in the day or enough days in the week. Finishing out the bathrooms in the pavilion consumed most Saturdays. Unfortunately, correcting errors consumed much of our time, like the night we spent chipping the cement away from the bathroom floor drains after the slab had been poured incorrectly, to enable standing water to flow into the drainpipe. On other Saturdays, "day campers" came from College Station or Bryan. Jennifer valiantly planned and led amazing inspirational programs for them. Scott, Nina, and I were her trusty assistants. Carol turned out to be a professional chef and always pitched in by volunteering to whip up great food on the grill or griddle, since there was no kitchen.

Sunday afternoons were usually spent working on our house. People had been generous with their time in helping us build the pavilion, and we were grateful. But Cross Roads was far from being all that it could be, and the four of us were exhausted.

We desperately needed help.

Catacombs

One Saturday, a fall mist cloaked the top of the trees. There was a slight chill in the moist air. Jennifer needed a Catacombs built for a program she was putting together about the early Christians, and quite frankly, we were out of steam. A group of junior high kids from an area church had agreed to assist in building the Catacombs for a service project, both to help us out and to reduce the fee for their retreat. Although the reduced fee didn't cover our cost, the kids provided much appreciated manpower.

The plan was to spend the morning making a cave by closing in a stretch of dry gully. Then after lunch Jennifer would lead them through the Catacombs program.

Throughout the morning the adult counselors toiled enthusiastically alongside the teenagers, cutting down small cedars and other saplings with clippers and machetes. For some of these kids, this was their first time to experience brushwork that didn't entail painting. They loved it. They yanked and pulled, stripping branches off of their stalks then dragging the stalks to the gully to form an A-frame over the trench. Branches were then laid over the stalks, forming a pitched roof over a twenty-foot length of the gully.

It was nice inside, dark and cave-like.

By lunch the mist was long gone. In its place a dazzling sun shone in a brilliant sky. Jackets littered the ground as the thermometer edged toward eighty degrees. We'd worked up quite an appetite that morning, and just as we finished, the aroma of barbeque wafted through the air. As we gathered up the tools and our jackets, Carol rang the big black dinner bell. *Clang, Clang, Clang, Clang!*

"Come 'n get it!" She yelled.

The kids stampeded for the delicious brisket that John Meckel, the elementary school principal, had volunteered to cook and deliver for nearly every retreat. We washed down the mouth-watering beef, garlic chive potatoes, green beans and, of course, Carol's secret recipe chocolate chunk brownies, with a gallon or two of lemonade.

After a short break, Jennifer called the group back together. She explained how the early Christians had been persecuted and had to worship in secret. She demonstrated the signs and symbols Christians had used to identify each other, such as a fish (the Icarus) or a dove. She showed pictures of the real Catacombs in Jerusalem and talked about the painted symbols that still remain on the sides of the caves to this day, symbols that let others know where the fugitive Christians met to worship. Soon she had the kids brainstorming scriptures and Bible stories, explaining that the early Christians had no Bibles and had to rely on their memories.

Then each camper painted a flat rock with a Christian symbol of his or her choice. Leaving the pavilion single file, we tramped silently down the narrow wooded trail to our newly erected Catacombs. Sitting solemnly inside the dark "cave," lit only by the flames of small candles gripped tightly in their hands, they shared all of the scriptures and Bible stories they could recall. Only the flickering light reflected in their eyes betrayed the excitement they felt by experiencing the dangerous, uniting reality faced by the early Christians. Finally, they left their rocks embedded in the cave wall to show others they had been there before them.

Everyone walked back to the camp humbled and inspired by the experience. Days like these kept us going.

House Angel

The dampness of that early morning transformed into a hot and muggy night. We were all spent, but Jennifer was so exhausted that she holed up in her bedroom, the only room with air conditioning. In her "delicate" condition, and after all she'd done that day, she more than deserved it.

The rest of us settled down in the tiny living room to watch our one TV channel. The only reason we could get that single channel was because Scott had climbed way, way up in a tree and nailed the antenna to a high limb. Television was not a priority in our lives.

Our priority to the point of obsession was the camp. The cabins so generously donated remained empty shells. Money and manpower were needed to run electric wire for lights and plugs, hang insulation, sheetrock, tape, float, texture, and paint. Unfortunately, there was still no money and little time, much less energy, to finish out the interiors. So the cabins sat fallow, their potential taunting us every time we drove by.

Working on our cottage was teaching me to hang light fixtures and ceiling fans while balanced atop a shaky ladder. I was also learning to cut, nail, and texture sheetrock using the "stomp 'n' drag" technique. That's where you fill a mop with gooey plaster, daub big messy patches over the sheetrock while it drips in your hair, then follow up by dragging a squeegee over it to lay down the little plaster tufts. God has such a sense of humor. He had used the experience with the farmhouse to teach us what we needed to know to finish out the cabins. Finding the time and money was another story.

Jennifer was understandably concerned about not having room for a proper nursery. The mess we called home was okay for us, but not for a baby. Cramming a pregnant woman in any house with her obsessed mother and teenage sister was a prescription for disaster, and my first grandchild was doing her part in making life difficult for the new momma-to-be.

The cramped and uncomfortable living conditions even made good sleep hard to come by. Many nights I tossed and turned on sheets turned gritty by sand filtering through the open windows. Getting ready for my sales job and trying to look professional was a daily challenge in that hot, sandy, crowded environment. The grueling work and constant demands on our time continued taxing our spirits and our dispositions. In the evenings, after my day job ended, I was too exhausted to think about fundraising or house hunting.

Nevertheless, Nina and I knew we needed to find a way to give Scott and Jennifer some time for themselves before the baby arrived. Scott located reputable house movers this time, in advance, which encouraged me to find a house before my money ran out. We passed out flyers all over Burleson County, scoured want ads, and put the word out among our friends. Weeks passed with no results, while the atmosphere at home deteriorated rapidly. We kept plodding along. Saturday: work on the camp or host a group of campers. Sunday: attend church then work on the house. Monday through Friday: hurry to work or school, then tackle paperwork, a newsletter, fundraising, marketing, or fixing a broken faucet.

One Saturday, all four of us tackled the task of covering exposed insulation in the bathroom walls of the new pavilion. Jen and I used a table saw to cut long inch-wide strips of cedar. She stood on one side of the saw, pushing the board toward me. The teeth of the spinning blade bit into the wood, creating a shrill, earsplitting whine. As the split board came my way I guided it to avoid binding the saw and burning up the motor, then Nina took the cedar strips to Scott, and together they nailed them over the slits between the wallboards.

The whirring of the saw drowned out the sound of an arriving truck, so we were surprised to see a middle-aged lady in overalls and a work shirt walk in. I'd met Bobbie Allen once at an Emmaus function, but I really didn't know her and had no idea what she was doing here. We stopped the saw to say hello.

"I lie around on the couch most Saturdays, watching cartoons, and eating cereal," she told us. "But today God wouldn't leave me alone until I came out to see for myself what you all are doing."

We welcomed her and handed her a hammer. As we labored side by side, Bobbie shared with us that she was divorced, her kids grown, and she was employed at the State School in Brenham. Her occupation was difficult and emotionally draining, which was why she "veged" on the couch most weekends.

We told her about Cross Roads, our hopes, and plans for its future, and shared some of the "God things" that had happened along the way.

"God has a habit of sending folks to help us," I said, setting the nails where she could reach them.

Then we told her we were looking for another house to move onto the property for Nina and me. Bobbie's hammer stopped in mid air, and her eyes grew round and wide.

"Now I know why God sent me here."

Mr. Rogers, a member who had lived across the street from the First United Methodist Church in Somerville, had passed away and left his home to the church."The church council voted just yesterday to put the house up for auction to be moved," Bobbie said. "They need to clear the lot for a new parsonage." It turned out that Mr. Rogers was also the grandfather of the Spiritual Director during my Walk to Emmaus. A coincidence?

We literally threw down our tools and bounded into the Suburban. Giddy with nervous anticipation of what God might have in store for us this time, we followed Bobbie to Somerville, to a quiet street tucked away from the main thoroughfare. On a corner sat a charming white 1920s home. Brick-lined concrete steps led to an inviting porch with square white wood columns atop massive brick supports.

My heart thumped with excitement, then abruptly sank.

"This is too nice," I whispered to Jennifer. "I can't afford this."

> *"This weekend God revealed many things to me about His plan for my life and His plan for the world. The Spirit of God is very strong in this place."*
>
> — Dora

I was learning to listen for His voice, however it might come.

CHAPTER 16

He Speaks in Many Ways

I did not want to go into that house. After our previous experiences pricing houses to be moved, I knew just from the lovely exterior that this one was way beyond my meager finances. I didn't want to get my hopes up. But Jennifer encouraged me.

"We're here, Mom. Let's just look at it."

The Somerville house

I stepped through the door onto avocado green, or maybe brown, shag carpet. All of the windows in the dimly lit house were covered with multiple layers of blinds, sheers, and various patterns of heavy brocade draperies. Moving through the living and dining area, which was one long room, we entered the kitchen, and I laughed.

"Look at those cabinets! Straight out of the nineteen-fifties."

They were white with yellow trim. The counter tops were red speckled Formica. Black and white vinyl tiles covered the floor.

A door at the rear of the kitchen opened onto a back porch that had been converted into a utility room. Mr. Rogers had nailed empty thread spools on every square inch of wall space in that room to hang his "gimme" hats.

"The floor plan's great, and it has three bedrooms," Jennifer said, sounding awestruck.

I felt the same way. The house wasn't big but compared to our cramped quarters at home; it was a mansion. I loved the solid wood doors with their crackling paint, the crystal doorknobs, the antique sugar-glass windows. Somewhere under that green-brown shag I suspected oak floors would be hiding.

"There's absolutely no way I can afford this house," I said, wishing it weren't so. "But since it's obvious that God led me to it, should we see how far He'll take it?"

Jennifer laughed with me and shrugged.

I had $10,000 left to my name. Chuck, the tough hands on owner of Central House Movers, quoted me $7,000 to cut the structure in half, "drop" the roof so it wouldn't hit the underpass between Somerville and Chriesman, move everything, and roughly put the house back together again.

"We'll need to cut through the shingles and fold back two sections of roof," Chuck said. "The fireplace, chimney, and front porch will have to come off." His experience and confidence was obvious and reassuring.

Rebuilding the fireplace, chimney, and porch was not included in the price, nor was re-shingling the roof. We'd have to do that part ourselves.

Chuck was reputable, so at least I knew he'd do his part right. But $7,000? That left only $3,000 to pay for the house. No way would it go for $3,000. But that's all I had, so I submitted my bid, trusting God to show me how to drum up money for the reconstruction, if our puny bid miraculously won out.

Busy Hands, Busy Minds

For two months I was a basket case, anxiously waiting for the church to notify the winning bidder. Fortunately, with our frenetic schedule, I actually had little time to fret. We were determined to finish the cabins for overnight campers by spring.

My friend, Mary, hosted a jumbo garage sale in the Baker Exploration parking lot in College Station, where she worked. She collected items from all over the Brazos Valley. Her garage sale raised $1,200, and after other folks chipped in with monetary donations, we finally had enough money to finish out the cabins and ready the camp for overnight retreats.

Over the next two months we scheduled several volunteer workdays. Together, we stapled rolls of insulation between the two-by-fours in the walls and ceiling, cut and nailed sheet rock over it, then taped, floated, textured and painted.

Volunteer Workday

At long last, the cabins were done.

One evening we were sitting in our "crooked little cottage," exhausted but exhilarated and thankful. Despite the fact that the camp's cabins had no beds or other furnishings, they represented a significant milestone that for a long while had seemed unlikely to ever happen. Life at Cross Roads was definitely looking up.

Jennifer, having left her purse in the car, asked Scott to go out and get it. He returned, purse tucked under his arm as he unfolded a crumpled flyer that was stuck to the bottom of it.

"What's that?" Jennifer said, pointing to the flyer.

"An advertisement." Scott studied it. "For an auction this Saturday at A&M."

Apparently, Texas A&M University was refurbishing a block of dorms and selling off the old furnishings. He read the list of auction items. "Hey, they have bunk beds!"

We had so little money. Why couldn't the auction have been a month or two later, after we had time to replenish our coffers? Besides, Scott and Jennifer were going to Austin that weekend to visit his father and step-mom. All around, the timing seemed impossible.

But solid oak bunk beds? I had to check it out.

After Scott and Jennifer left, Nina and I spent a long night alone in the house. We sat in the middle of the living room floor, a shotgun clutched between us, listening to a pack of coyotes howl through the open windows. We were positive they had the house surrounded. When Saturday morning rolled around, I was gladly off to College Station. A few hours into the sale, the auctioneer came to the bunk beds. The bidding began at $10, then $20, $50, $100.

"Going once, twice, three times... *sold* to Hilda Hellums," the auctioneer yelled.

I'd won! We couldn't afford many sets at a hundred dollars each, but at eighty percent less than the catalogue versions, I had to buy a few.

I collected myself to bid on the next set, but the auctioneer moved on to the desks. Perplexed, I turned to a fellow bidder.

"Why isn't he auctioning off the rest of the beds?"

"Ma'am, you bought the whole lot," the man said. "One hundred bunk bed sets for one hundred dollars."

I nearly fainted. Enough beds for both cabins and then some.

My joy turned to panic when I learned that I had to take them all home before the end of the day. Where could I muster the help I needed? From my friends at church, of course. Friends showed up with horse trailers and trucks, and by evening the bunks were unloaded safely, if a little haphazardly, in the new cabins.

This experience had been eye opening all around. I'd never come away from a sale feeling so elated, and I'd never known God to advertise in flyers, especially one stuck to the bottom of a purse. Maybe He was having fun with me. At any rate, I was learning to listen for His voice however it might come.

*Therefore I tell you, whatever you ask for in prayer, believe that
you have received it, and it will be yours.* - Matthew 11:24

CHAPTER 17

Home Again, Home Again

A few nights later as we sat watching TV together, a real estate ad
came on. Staring straight at me, a man adamantly shook his finger
and yelled, "You got your house!"

A warm glow and a sense of peace came over me. All the
anxiety I'd felt waiting for the church to call drained away. I knew
the house I'd bid on in Somerville was mine.

Sure enough, a few days later the Somerville church called
to confirm it.

"Ms. Hellums? You were the highest bidder ..." I didn't need
to hear the rest: The house was mine. My prayers, the prayers of
my friends and our little family were answered.

After the joyous thrill of winning subsided a bit, I told Scott
and Jennifer I wanted them to have the new house. It was bigger
than the one we were living in and would be better for them and
the new baby. Nina and I would do fine in the cottage.

They wouldn't take it. I can't imagine why, and never got an
explanation.

Winter Rains

We bought the house in the fall. Although Scott had been smart to find reputable movers well in advance, we soon discovered that the number of houses to be moved far outnumbered the days available to the few movers in the area. We were put on a waiting list. By the time our turn came, it was winter and had started to rain. Rules and regulations prevented moving a house in inclement weather.

Meanwhile, our little family continued suffering from too much togetherness. Four people in a space the size of a small apartment were often three too many. When we moved there from the rental house in Chriesman, I'd put all my furniture in storage, except for my bed. Scott and Jennifer's furniture was wall-to-wall in our tiny living area. Even our clothes were crowded, because houses built back then had no closets.

So we were popping out at the seams. Our pet goats, Dave and Judy, were still poking their heads up through the floorboards, and the house seemed to be getting smaller by the day. Jennifer was getting bigger and bigger every day.

Her pregnancy was not an easy one. She was borderline toxemic. She bloated up, retained fluids, suffered with backaches, and she was still teaching fourth grade. All day she'd deal with screaming children, then at night she didn't get a lot of rest. In the evenings, we tried to take care of her, make her as comfortable as possible. We made hot compresses by filling crew socks with Uncle Ben's, and putting them in the microwave for her neck and back. Many nights, to preserve her sanity, Jennifer withdrew to her bedroom and read books or magazines.

Usually, Jennifer is outgoing and very social, but she was depressed during those months. Here she was, living in a miserable dump in the middle of nowhere, expecting her first baby. Who would want to bring a child into such a situation? She wasn't raised that way.

We'd lived through some tough times, but we always had a nice home in a nice neighborhood. These living conditions were new for all of us. Jennifer didn't mind for herself, but after she got pregnant, she minded because of the baby.

The room that should have been the baby's nursery was her mom's bedroom. Money was short. They were living on her teacher's salary. Every day that passed, Jennifer became more and more depressed.

Scott, proud first father, also felt bad about bringing a baby into that situation. He wanted everything to be perfect for his first child, so he was working double time, completely task oriented, to make the house as livable as possible. This meant Jennifer wasn't getting her husband's attention, causing her to feel neglected.

Temporary Quarters

My friend Cindy VanDeventer had a mobile home on her property, which she had moved out of after buying a new one. Her mother-in-law occasionally stayed there when she came to visit, but otherwise the spare home sat vacant. I asked Cindy if Nina and I could live there temporarily, until my house arrived.

"We're on top of each other," I confided. "And it would be for only a month or two, at the most."

"Of course you can," Cindy said, after consulting her husband.

A mental and moral burden lifted from my shoulders. My Angel on Wheels had come through again. I hugged her gratefully.

"My friend, you don't know how much this will help. Our family has been stressed right up to the breaking point."

Nina and I moved the necessities to our temporary quarters. We had plenty of room to spread out, leaving Scott and Jennifer more room, as well. Unfortunately, a "month or two" stretched and stretched as we waited our turn on the movers' schedule. Every time our turn came, it would be raining in our area, and we'd go back on the list. I knew we were overstaying our welcome, although Cindy was much too good a friend to ever mention it.

One Tough Group

People who come to Texas from the north often scoff at our version of winter. They talk of being snowed in for months or of subzero temperatures. But when a long, hard Texas winter finally comes along, they sing a much different tune. Instead of snow, we get bucket-loads of rain, sleet, wind and occasionally hail, which makes for a damp bone chilling cold even at thirty degrees.

Our first overnight campers came during a bitter cold period that winter, and they weren't prepared for the weather, much less the truly rustic conditions they encountered. The cabins were heated, of course, but meals were served and meetings were held in the outdoor open-air pavilion. I saw history repeating itself, as their faces reflected the exact expression I must have worn at my first retreat.

Oh, my gosh, what are we doing here? they seemed to be thinking.

That first overnight group tried to stay cooped up in their cabin, for the most part, which was very disappointing. This was an important milestone for us, and we desperately wanted these kids to experience Cross Roads at its best during their weekend.

They'd come for the purpose of strengthening their sense of community. During the program, we went overboard showering them with God's love, trying to show them Christ in everyday, not always perfect, circumstances. After all, Cross Roads is a place for shedding worldly comforts and embracing God in the simplicity of nature. We attempted to show them that only through loving, giving, and sharing is a person going to find joy regardless of their situation. It's all about attitude. A Christ-like attitude.

By the time the weekend was over, our new friends were like a big family and were not ready to leave. A spirit filled camaraderie had developed among them despite the harsh environment.

That was a tough group and a tough weekend. The next group that came was blessed with much better weather, for which we were all extremely grateful.

Great Expectations

While Nina and I were living at Cindy's place, Jennifer and Scott turned their talents to creating a nursery for their first baby, spending every spare moment to make it ready in time. They painted the walls and ceiling cerulean blue, then glued glow-in-the-dark phosphorescent stars on the ceiling. In that dazzling night sky, they hung a pretty white ceiling fan then decorated the window shades with cutouts of a moon and stars. For a shelf, they painted a board white and attached it to the wall with ribbon. A colorful rug, a crib, and the rocking chair I had rocked Jennifer in finished it off.

In the midst of these renovations, two monumental events occurred. The first came by mail, the second by phone.

My mind on the zillion things that needed to be done, I stopped to check the mail. A manila business-size envelope stood out from all the others. The return address was the Internal Revenue Service. Ripping open the envelope, I held my breath.

The letter inside was dated January 22, 1998. It was the news we'd awaited for months, and thanks to our angel, Mr. Strube, the news was good: our 501(c)3 Tax Exempt Status had been granted! Amazingly, it was granted on our first submission.

The second monumental good news came in early March. The rains finally stopped and Chuck phoned to say our house would arrive at Cross Roads the following day.

This Old House

They had to cut it in half, of course, and they did a fine job putting it back together. But getting the house ready for move-in was another laborious, time-consuming production.

The kitchen had eight levels of vinyl flooring to be removed. Every night we got down on our hands and knees and scraped off layer after layer. That house had seen a lot of years come and go, and we could gauge the passage of time by each pattern of the vinyl. The final layer had been put down with tar over beautiful red oak floors.

We hired a professional floor man to scrape and sand them down, but he gave up after a day or two. It took us over a week just to scrape away all those layers, then we rented a floor sander to finish them. Nina sat on the sander for added traction and hung on for dear life while we pushed it around. The rest of the house had matted shag carpet, three layers thick, and I don't know how long the drapes had been on the windows. We pulled them down.

Where the fireplace had been removed was a seven-foot hole. We backed the "Ghost" up to this hole and shoved all the debris out into the truck bed. One day I stepped toward the bed of the truck, and as I lunged forward to toss in an armload of trash, the floor gave way. I spun backwards and fell more than four feet to the ground.

For a few minutes, I was afraid to move. Once you move, you know what's broken. Luckily, I didn't break anything, but for several days I was too sore to be much help.

Progress on the house seemed to go at a snail's pace. Scott managed to scrape together the needed materials, and many of our friends came out on weekends to help.

One day Cindy VanDeventer came to see me, crying. Her mother-in-law was coming for a visit, and they needed their mobile home. It broke Cindy's heart to tell me I had to leave. She didn't have a choice. And truly, I'd been at Cindy's much longer that I'd planned to be there.

But my house wasn't close to being ready.

> *"When you walk down that trail, it feels like God is with you."*
>
> – Sarah

God promises to finish what He starts: "... What I have said, that will I bring about; what I have planned, that will I do." – Isaiah 46:11

CHAPTER 18

Cross Walk

My house wasn't ready, but I moved in anyway. I felt as if my life had been in storage along with my worldly possessions. The last year and half had felt more like five years, and I couldn't wait to finally unpack my things. After all, my "new" old house had the necessities: a roof over my head, a bed to sleep in, food, electricity, and water. Isn't that all anyone really needs?

Our long uphill push was over. It was now just a matter of time before Jennifer and I could quit our secular jobs and devote our full attention to Cross Roads. The major pieces were in place for the camp, the tax exemption, two cabins and pavilion. We were officially nonprofit, and each of our two families had a house to live in. One house promised to be especially nice when the reconstruction was done, while the cottage would never be more than marginal at best. But Jennifer and Scott had a room for the baby now, and if our good fortune continued, one day they would build their dream house.

I'd scarcely moved in when it was time for Cross Roads' biggest event of the spring. Jennifer had been planning it all winter, praying it wouldn't be rained out. We'd enlisted many of our friends as "actors," and Scott was playing the biggest role of all.

Jennifer was fresh from her Emmaus Walk. While she'd found it encouraging, the physical discomfort of sitting through a three-day retreat of any kind and sleeping on bunks at night during her second trimester of pregnancy was exhausting. Nevertheless, she was excited about our group of campers coming in from Houston.

At seven p.m. the headlights of the caravan shone up the driveway. The leaders hopped out apologizing profusely for being late. Jennifer and Nina directed them to the cabins to unload. After a tumultuous thirty minutes, the excited, screaming teenagers finished exploring their new surroundings, dumped their baggage in the cabins, and like moths to a flame streaked toward the pavilion tables, where their counselors were piling a mountain of Cokes, chips, cookies, and snacks.

A breezy chill in the air that March evening accentuated the absence of walls. The kids didn't seem to notice as we called them together to begin the program.

Kick Off

Scott was up first. He welcomed the group to Cross Roads and, employing his impish sense of humor, he proceeded to instill the proper amount of respect in them for the surrounding woods.

"This is a wilderness area. Deer, coyotes, armadillos, raccoons, squirrels, wild hogs, and snakes live here."

Squeals of feigned terror and nervous giggles of delight rose from the group.

"This is their home. Kick any sticks before you pick them up to make sure they don't come alive and bite you. If you're on a trail that's fairly wide and you can stand up straight, then it's a trail we cut for people. If you have to bend over, we didn't make that trail. We don't know what did and have no idea where it might go. All one-hundred-and-sixty acres are fenced, so, if you get lost and find a fence, you can probably follow the fence to the front gate. And you might make it. But we have a better idea for you. If you do get lost, we ask you to stay put and yell 'bananas!'"

This time the kids broke out in whoops and laughter. "Bananas?!!"

"Why bananas? Because kids often scream 'help' when playing games, but if we hear 'bananas,' we'll know you're serious. Trust me, we haven't lost anyone yet and don't want to start now."

When Scott finished, it was Jennifer's turn to shine. She led the group in our trademark icebreaker, asking them to relate an object chosen randomly from the basket to their Christian life. One chose an eraser, and said it represented how Jesus erases your sin. Another picked out a paper clip and said it showed how Jesus helps you hold your life together. And so it went, until all the kids had chosen an object and shared their thoughts.

This exercise went over quite well. It was obvious that these high-schoolers were fairly mature in their faith. Watching them, I felt proud of my daughter and her husband, proud of the camp, thankful for this group who had joined us here, and certain that the Cross Walk program would be an inspirational experience for us all.

To wrap things up for the evening, I led a devotional about Lent. I shared that Lent was meant to be a time to slow down and focus on the sacrifice that Christ made for us, that it is only by joining Christ in the valley of His final days on earth that we can fully experience the miracle and joy of Easter. Leaving the kids to ponder on that, we said goodnight.

Full of excitement and anticipation of what the next day might bring, they headed for their cabins, while we headed for home to get some rest.

Come and Get It

The next morning we arose early and met Carol at the pavilion to fix breakfast for our twenty-five guests. Scott fried sausage patties on a griddle. Nina and I set out juices, coffee, cereal, milk, and fruit. Drawn by the aroma of perking coffee, the adult campers arrived at the pavilion first, and the kids trickled in soon after. I led them in a prayer, then as the hungry campers filed past, Jennifer and Scott flipped pancakes onto their plates. Some of the boys came back for seconds and even thirds.

Free time followed breakfast, giving us a break to hurriedly eat our own meal and clean up the dishes. By that time, the kids were jumping to get on with the days activities.

Jennifer passed out materials for each person to make a scratchy, sackcloth bracelet to wear as a reminder of Jesus' sacrifice. Then Jennifer led a discussion focused on Jesus' life as a child and teen. She included games and running the Obstacle Course, where the ending devotional questions dealt with the sacrifices we make for each other.

Afterward, Scott enlisted all their help in constructing a fifteen-foot cross. As they broke for lunch, their conversations bubbled with guesses about what Scott planned for them to do with that cross.

Cross Walk actors

Stories, Vignettes and Inspiration

Unknown to the campers, people had been gathering at my house all morning, getting into costume and practicing their lines. Scott was nervous and uncomfortable about the enormous responsibility of portraying Jesus. He was determined not to put any words in Jesus' mouth, to stick strictly with scripture whenever he spoke.

Appearing at the top of the hill in costume, Scott started the Living History "Walk with Jesus" by beckoning to the campers.

"Come, follow me," he called, and they ran to join him.

At each bend in the trail, Jennifer had designed a vignette inspired by scripture.

The healing of the leper, the fallen woman at the well, the faith of the Roman Centurion, the rich ruler, nimble Zaccheus the tax collector and the hapless moneychangers in the temple each portrayed enthusiastically by our wonderful friends.

I walked along as one of the throng of followers, so that I could lead a discussion between each station. I commented on how hot it was - and that it was even hotter in the Middle East. I remarked on the difficulty of trudging through deep sand, as Jesus had done so long ago, and offered our sweaty "Jesus" a drink of water. My role was to reveal Jesus' humanity.

One of the counselors was particularly moved by the portrayal of the Rich Young Ruler.

"Now I understand," she remarked to her peers. "That story isn't about hopelessness, it's about grace. It's about understanding there is *nothing* we can do to earn salvation. It's a gift."

I smiled as the warmth of the Holy Spirit welled up inside me.

After a break, the kids took turns silently carrying the cross to its resting place at the outdoor sanctuary. Scott helped them erect the cross, then led an exercise of self-examination, reflection, and prayer. One by one each person walked to the foot of the cross, where hot coals glowed in a small hibachi, and placed in the coals a scrap of paper. Written on the paper was a personal sacrifice, something to be given up.

I could see that these young people were taking the exercise quite seriously. As their paper burned, their whole countenance changed. They looked peaceful. When all were finished, the faces around the cross bore a few tears and a few smiles as they reverently watched the smoke of their offerings waft heavenward.

A man spoke, breaking the silence.

"My son died a few years ago." His voice faltered as he continued. "This weekend has renewed my faith."

Although I was tired to the bone, the sense of purpose and fulfillment I felt was gratifying and humbling. God promises to finish what He starts, and Christ had been with us this weekend as we witnessed the light of the Holy Spirit radiating from the individuals Christ had sent us to serve.

Lives had been changed.

"Dear Hilda, Carol and the Servants of God Thank you for showing us the meaning of Serving. You guys were such a true example of Christ's Servants. Your manners, cheerfulness, fruit of the Spirit was just flowing within and in your life... Your love for the Lord humbled me. Such a blessing... The Presence of God is so full in this place. May God bless your endeavors and your giving."

Daisy John

No matter how tired we were at the end of the week... those weekend retreat groups were the fuel that reignited us.

CHAPTER 19

The Year of Grace

March, April, and May are crucial months for a retreat camp. They promise the best weather for outdoor activities, and the world is naturally filled with the wonderment of new life.

Our spring at Cross Roads was packed with so much commotion that it passed in a hectic jumble. Every weekend both our houses were invaded by three or four people busily cooking three meals a day plus snacks.

And it was fun. When I was younger, I didn't want people dropping in on me because my house might not be perfect. I was too insecure to be a particularly social person, so I didn't have much company. Cross Roads changed all that. Cooking meals together was a communal endeavor, with Carol in charge bossing us around. I loved it.

I had changed jobs now and was selling auto glass during the week, something I'd successfully done before. Scott also had taken a job. With the baby coming and no money to work on their house, he had no choice. Scott's mother was a businesswoman, so he'd spent much of his formative years in daycare or with nannies.

He wanted Jennifer to be able to stay at home after the baby came. And Jennifer wanted that, too.

Cindy, my Angel on Wheels, got him a job where she was employed, at the Thrifty Nickel, as a part-time designer putting together their ads. Scott worked there two days a week, until he heard about a fulltime graphic design position at Texas A&M.

After two years at Cross Roads, we realized that building the camp was an ongoing project that might never be completely finished. There would always be one more thing we could add and always something to fix. When we first came, we expected to get a loan and build the camp immediately. The income would support us all, we believed, and if not, Scott would go back to work. Not a bad strategy, even though it hadn't played out that way.

I knew God's plan was destined to work out in the end, but the going was much slower and more difficult than I'd ever imagined it would be. With the three of us working day jobs, serving the groups on the weekends, and construction still necessary on the camp, we had little time or energy left to make my house livable, even though I was earning money now and could invest in materials. Fortunately, the weather was fair, so the lack of air conditioning wasn't yet a problem. In the hole where the fireplace had been, I'd placed a screen from a sliding patio door to keep the bugs out. That would do until I could afford to have the chimney rebuilt.

I wanted an old-fashioned chimney and fireplace, not the modern version that starts with a kit. This was a period house, and I wanted the chimney to fit the period, but not many bricklayers know how to build one anymore. Scott had managed to track down a brick mason who was a true master of his craft, but the man was getting on in years and only worked for brief periods. Once again, I was on a waiting list, this time praying I'd have the money when my turn came.

Surprisingly, no matter how tired we were at the end of the week, or how much we dreaded getting ready for the next crowd of kids to arrive on Friday night, those weekend retreat groups provided the spark that reignited us. Yes, we had to rush home from our day jobs then work late into the night preparing for their arrival, knowing we'd be up early Saturday morning to cook breakfast and start the program. But within an hour after the kids arrived, we were having fun together, getting to know one another, and by the time the weekend was over, we had thirty new best friends. No matter how exhausted we were on Sunday afternoon, we were always sad to see them go. The weekend groups kept us going. They gave purpose to our lives. Everything else was tough, but watching the Holy Spirit work miracles every weekend made it more than worth the effort.

Circle up

Grace in the Muddle

Our plan was to spend the following summer, when weekend groups wouldn't be coming to Cross Roads, completing our various incomplete structures. We also expected to have a new baby before then.

Jennifer was ready. Her due date had come and gone.

"April Fool's Day? Can't you wait another week?" I asked her.

"No." Her pregnancy was difficult, and she wanted it over. "My doctor has that date available, so we're inducing."

I understood how she felt, but what child would want to be born on April Fool's Day? I could just imagine cardboard birthday cakes and trick presents. At least, it was a beautiful time of the year.

The hospital waiting room and halls were clogged with excited relatives waiting to welcome the first grandchild on either side of the family. Grace's birth proved to be just as difficult as the pregnancy. After what seemed like forever, Jennifer was rushed from labor to delivery. A short time later, Grace made her debut from behind the nursery window, cradled in the arms of her beaming dad.

Both families were lined up, staring in wonder at the precious new life. Jennifer and Scott had named her Grace Anne.

"Oooooh, look how cute."

"She's adorable."

"Ahhhhh, what a sweetie."

"I think she looks like ...." The chorus went on and on.

The first gift that awaited Grace was a purple Princess Diana beanie baby. My mother had entered Jennifer's name in a drawing at the hospital gift shop. Two blue-haired ladies had come right in the middle of Jennifer's labor to declare her the winner.

Comes the Long, Hot Summer

My first grandchild, a darling, sweet baby girl, lived at my house as much as at her parents' house. Scott's paternal grandparents hooked up their travel trailer, and stayed to take care of the girls while we were at work. At night, Scott and I helped out as much as possible.

Jennifer recovered quickly and returned to work in time for the last week of school. After that she stayed home with her new daughter. Progress on the camp, and our houses, was put on hold while we all adjusted to and reveled in life with Grace.

One evening, a battered work truck pulled up to the house. A weathered old man in faded jeans and a flannel shirt climbed out. The stub of a cigarette was tightly pinched between his gnarled thumb and forefinger.

"Ma'am, are you ready for your fireplace?" he asked, waving the glowing cigarette stub.

This must be Mr. Kluge, the brick mason. My day was unexpectedly blessed.

Watching him craft that fireplace and chimney brick by brick was a marvel. We experienced an artistic process that most people of our generation, and generations to come, will only read about in books.

As summer approached, with the Texas heat rising steadily, fans did little more than push the hot air around. Jennifer and Scott decided one day while I was at work to install an air conditioner in my house. It was a window unit, and the hole for it was up high on the living room wall. As they were trying to lift the heavy unit into place, it slipped and landed on Scott's ankle.

After hours of excruciating pain sitting in the emergency room and waiting for X-rays, Scott sat with Jennifer, the pain relievers finally taking effect. The doctor came in and pronounced his injury a torn tendon.

"Don't plan on going anywhere without crutches for a while," he told my son-in-law. "This will take quite a time to heal."

Scott's plans for the summer shattered as he realized he'd be confined to his recliner, with a new baby to care for and an itchy cast.

The world has yet to see what God can do with and for and through and in a man who is fully and wholly consecrated to Him. - Revivalist Henry Varley

CHAPTER 20

A Tough Texas Winter

Scott's youngest sister, a quiet, shy, and inquisitive sixteen-year-old, was twelve years his junior. She came down from Dallas to help care for him and Grace, while Jennifer stepped in to take over Scott's outdoor responsibilities. I know Scott was frustrated about all the work that needed doing, work that only he could do, yet he could do little more than crutch around and try to accomplish simple tasks one-handed while balancing on one foot.

The good news was that Scott used his down time to design a new brochure and a newsletter. Word of mouth about Cross Roads was kicking in, too. By September, he was mastering crutches and a walking cast, and we had packed our calendar with incoming retreats. Weekends off became few and far between.

Every fee collected we funneled back into the camp for resources. We purchased supplies for Jennifer's programs, cedar for an outdoor sanctuary, cast iron pots for campfire cooking, and garbage cans. We started a building fund for enclosing the pavilion and for constructing Carol's dream kitchen. Her days volunteering as a "chuck-wagon cook" would soon be over.

With money for our years of effort finally coming in, instead of always draining out, our spirits and enthusiasm recharged. If bookings continued at this rate, we'd soon be back on our financial feet by the time Scott was completely healed and his little sister was back in Dallas.

Change in Plans

Fall passed in a blur. One group after another, each with its own personality, arrived on Friday evenings. Regardless of how difficult our workweek had been, we did our best to greet them with joy and optimism and share with them a deeper understanding of God's blessings. On most Sunday mornings, after we served breakfast to the campers, I hurried off to Sunday school and church. The women in my Sunday school class were so encouraging and supportive that I really hated to miss a class.

One cold, drizzly December afternoon I was changing my church clothes before going down to the camp to clean up after our weekend guests, when Jeremy called. During the years he'd been gone, Jeremy occasionally came home to Cross Roads to help us with a retreat. He was a natural, having been a counselor at Camp ChoYeh for several summers, and he loved working with kids. But today, he wasn't calling about helping out.

"Mom, Tina and I want to get married."

I was shocked, of course, but not entirely surprised. Tina McCollum was Jeremy's high school sweetheart.

"Now?" I asked, wondering what had spurred their sudden decision. Tina's goal for as long as they'd known each other was to go to college at Southern Methodist University in Dallas and to get a degree. She'd made the Dean's list her first semester. How did marriage fit that plan?

"We might wait until summer for the wedding," Jeremy said, "but she's coming home with me for Christmas break."

As it turned out, Tina was in crisis. Her parents wanted her to leave SMU, live with them, and go to college in Houston, so they refused to sign her junior year financial aid forms. They'd always disliked Jeremy, and would probably dislike anyone who tried to "steal" their only child. When Jeremy invited Tina to his sister's wedding, they refused to let her attend until I phoned and promised that I would "look after Tina exactly as I would if she were my own daughter." They were good people, but they kept Tina on a very tight leash.

Now Tina was devastated about having to give up her dream of getting her degree at SMU, so she and Jeremy had decided to marry, which would free her of her parents' control. I was sad about the circumstances behind the kids' decision, but extremely happy for them. They'd been in love for many years and were obviously made for each other.

When Tina came home with Jeremy that Christmas, we began making plans for an August wedding. I had no idea how I would be able to give them the wedding they deserved. Even though the camp was booked solid, it didn't pay us anything. We had no extra money, no time, and working seven days a week, no energy left to give. Somehow, I knew God would provide.

Another Texas Winter

January brought freezing weather along with a group of about twenty-five teenagers and adults. The group arrived Friday evening just as a full moon crested the treetops and floated slowly up into the clear night sky. Saturday morning broke to icy cold wind and rain. It was the kind of weather that turned our clay driveway into hazardous mush and any weekend retreat into survival of the fittest.

Carol arrived at our houses early to throw a pan of her special breakfast tacos in the oven. While they baked, we piled into my

Suburban and headed to the open air pavilion, where we set up coffee and hot chocolate to tide the kids over until we could start dishing out the food.

The teenagers were huddled together under the pavilion's roof like penguins on an ice floe. Against all advice, the young women had come to the camp dressed in shorts and flip-flops, and the young men weren't dressed much warmer. It seemed no one had brought a coat. They stood warming their hands around cups of coffee or hot chocolate, shaking miserably.

We ran home to comb our closets for every available sweater, jacket, or sweatshirt we could find, and loaded them into the Suburban. As soon as the tacos were ready, Carol jerked them out of the oven and shoved in briskets for dinner that night. When we arrived back at the pavilion, the kids actually went for the clothes before the food, which was a first.

While they ate, we built a bonfire for them to warm up by, and after a hot meal, the kids felt better. Then the group retreated into their heated cabins for the remainder of the day. Jennifer hastily redesigned her program for use indoors and joined them.

This was the first time we'd been aware that Cross Roads was completely inadequate to the needs of our campers. We were used to "roughing it," but this group had clearly expected, and required, an indoor dining and meeting facility.

For lunch, Carol presented them with a choice of grilled chilidogs or Frito pie. For dinner we took her fabulous briskets, which had been cooking in our ovens all day, along with butter-and-chive potatoes, baked beans, bread, and all the fixings down to the campers. We did our best to make them as comfortable as possible, but we were pretty sure they wouldn't be back.

After dinner, shivering in the cold ourselves, we loaded up the dinner dishes and headed home. Just as we made the turn up to our houses, the Suburban sank in the muddy red clay.

Exhausted, disheartened, and miserable with cold, four of us got out to push, while Nina took the wheel. Teeth chattering, freezing rain soaking our clothes, spinning tires spewing muck in our faces, we rocked the vehicle back and forth until it finally slid forward. Then we jumped in, not caring a bit that we were all muddy messes. We just wanted to go home.

Further Disheartenment

Jennifer and Scott's cottage was proving to be a money pit, and their money was running out. Scott worked on my house more than theirs, because I had more resources for buying materials. Translation: my credit cards weren't maxed out yet.

The cottage bathroom was in dire need of remodeling. It was an add-on to the original structure and had barely survived the move. A tiny sink dangled from the wall. The tub wobbled unsteadily with any movement. An opening over the tub, which at one time had been an outdoor window, now existed as a square hole in the interior wall separating the bathroom from Jennifer and Scott's bedroom. We'd covered it with plywood on one side and a shower curtain on the other, to keep water from running down inside the wall, a makeshift solution at best.

Grace, approaching her first birthday and increasingly mobile, badly needed a safe yard to play in during good weather. Bull nettle, thorns, scorpions, and snakes lurked just outside the doors waiting for her curious little mind and hands to check them out. Confining her to the house was impossible and frustrating, but necessary.

Cross Roads, despite our wonderfully packed fall schedule, wasn't going to support us anytime soon. We had reached a plateau, where all our energy was being poured into working our full-time jobs and attending the retreat groups, and all our earnings were being poured right back into the camp. Without a major infusion of cash, the cycle couldn't be broken.

Cross Roads is definitely God's country. There's no doubt about it. The Holy Spirit lives here. I didn't know that when I moved to Chriesman twenty-two years ago. The land up the road from me was just land. The dirt road was like a scrub board, and the turnaround was my driveway. Nobody lived past me.

But I must have sensed the goodness here. When I moved, I was trying to get away from everybody, trying to protect my boys. I didn't want anything bad or evil coming around them. I was like a mama bear, and these were my cubs.

Carol Moreland (left), and her sister, Debbie Batts

Then Hilda moved in up the road. Here's this city person, got her makeup on half the time. Never held a hammer, never swung a machete. Now she's got a chain saw. Lord, help her, *I thought,* don't let her cut her legs off.

Hilda had her kids, all from the big city, too. Everybody wanted to work, wanted to do stuff. They had their headbands tied around their heads, or around their necks to keep the sweat from rolling down their backs. Hilda's kids were like little dynamos, go, go, go. I had to make sure they rested, stopped and drank water. Sit down, take a break, eat a sandwich, then go, go, go, go, go, until it was dark and they couldn't see.

And this was every day. It'd be hot. This is Texas. I'd been living out here a while, working to keep my place going. I know what that heat can do to you. It will put you down quick. It can do serious damage to your body.

Work is good, but it gets old. I'd say, " Let's just sit down here and vegetate a while."

It's amazing what people thought out here. There're still people to this day who don't know what Cross Roads is. They see sixty cars leaving down this little road on a Saturday night, and they're wondering what in the world is going on up here. Nowadays, when you pass four cars, you wonder where are all these cars coming from? Back when I first moved here, you didn't pass anybody. Then they gave us pavement, so now we have more cars.

We had a little house, me and the boys, and we heated it with a cast iron Ben Franklin fireplace, so we needed a lot of firewood come winter. When all those trees were knocked down on your road, my son said, "There's a girl that lives there named Nina."

There weren't too many people out here, not as many as now, and I'd heard things from neighbors about that bunch of hippies.

"Carol, you need to stay away from there," people told me.

"Well, I'm getting firewood," I told them.

Then I met Hilda. I was surprised. Hadn't known what to expect, but I saw the vision God had inspired in her and what she was trying to achieve. I volunteered my boys, thought this would give them an opportunity to do something good, learn how to clear land, build up their self-esteem being around a man like Scott. There was no male in my family except the boys. I was a chef up at A&M, and felt like I worked all the time. This would be good for them.

God's hand was in all of it. I just didn't know it then.

In Austin I was a big shot for years, had my own restaurant and catering business, featured in the Austin Home & Garden, new upcoming chef. Later I was chef at A&M, raising three boys on my own out in the woods. And I was not brought up in the woods. In my day, you had men's work and you had women's work. Chopping wood was not women's work. You stayed in the house. I didn't know anybody when I moved to Texas, didn't even know what Texas looked like. Then my journey started, and it brought me to Cross Roads.

The big barn raising was awesome. That was the first time we ever got the food together for me to be the chef at Cross Roads. There's always food. God provides.

Cooking is not Hilda's expertise, so she was thrilled. After working full time all week, being a chef, it's not an easy job. I was on my feet all day, then came out here to cook. He just kept me going. It's amazing how you come to life when you get here. You can be double-dog tired at home. Try to talk yourself out of it. Once I come, I'm glad to be here.

There was always something special here at this camp. I felt it every time I came on to this land. I was in and out, in and out, like I still am. Down these roads and paths here at the camp. It's a feeling. The Holy Spirit. Everybody who came for that barn raising, they felt it, too.

Then the men came from Austin, from The Journey of Imperfect Faith. A team came in a day early to preview the camp, check it out. It was perfect. They wanted to walk the paths, pray over the camp, and start developing the camp to their theme. Grown men. I didn't know men were so spiritual.

We had just built the conference room. The cement on the fireplace was still wet. A couple of rocks fell off and had to be put back on later. The cedar on the walls was still real cedary, sealed, but freshly done. We were doing the hustle so this would be ready for the group.   Then they started bringing in trailers. They carried in couches, tapestry, rugs, pictures, these were Christian pictures in beautiful frames as tall as me, and I'm five-foot-nine. I swear they took them out of their church. They brought water fountains. Tranquil singing music. They totally changed the conference room. It was like a step into heaven.

The men for the conference came that evening, and the team had done tiki torches all the way up the road, and the path coming down to the camp. I watched from a distance. I was spellbound.

They kept the bonfire going for four days, brought in trailers of wood. We'll do the first fire, but after that it's up to the group. This was autumn, cool.

For their talks, they stretched out a sheet and used a projector. The presence of the Holy Spirit was overwhelming. I didn't want to leave. I wanted to be a fly on the wall.

We've had all the churches at Cross Roads. We bring them together in fellowship, and God uses us. I don't think we've ever had a group that left unhappy. I don't think we've ever had a group that wasn't moved or changed by Cross Roads, by the Holy Spirit at Cross Roads. It isn't you, it isn't me. He uses us, just as he uses this camp.

It's awesome how God uses Cross Roads to relieve and renew. We all have problems. If you're going to walk in the light, it's not an easy walk. But God uses everybody who comes out here.

Hundreds of volunteers come through here to work in the kitchen. I remember one girl who was coming here to help out *at seven in the morning. She didn't know where she was going, but went to where she saw some cars parked. Still pretty dark, so she had a flashlight. Walked into the kitchen and said she felt the presence of the Holy Spirit there. The sounds and smells of cooking, the praise music on the little jam box.*

We greeted her, "Hey, how you doing, we're glad to have you."

This was her first encounter behind the walls of Cross Roads. Before we started cooking together, we prayed, because we need God to do his work through us. And this made a lasting impression on her. First you pray, then cook, getting to know each other. And we're liable to break out singing at any moment.

When it's serving time, you come up through the line to the hot food. You pass several long tables, lavish with fruits, muffins, cereals and oatmeal, with all the blueberries and other trimmings to go with it. Then you've got the coffee table at the other end. A banquet.

The way I see it, we're serving the heirs to the Throne. And when you're serving royalty, you take the extra step, do a little extra. Everybody's happy to be there, with the love of Christ flowing like a visible river.

I became the Minister of Meals. MOM. I'm always ministering to people with my mom skills, making sure everyone's comfortable. Little did I know God had plans for me to be a mom all my life on Earth, with the children who come through the camp. All the men who come through the camp and miss their moms. All the women who come through the camp and would like a minute with their mom.

The groups at the camp, it's just awesome to see them come together. I really enjoy seeing the kids who come here and how God works with them.

I worked at the university, around college kids, right out of the nest and a little crazy. It's all about them. But that's better than when I worked in a high school. At lunchtime, fights broke out. You were in fear of their lives, in fear of your life. I got a bad outlook on kids. They scared me. I didn't understand.

I thought, What is this country going to be when these are the leaders of our churches, the leaders of our country? There are no good kids. Look at 'em. Look how they dress, listen to the trash coming out of their mouths, look how they're fighting, going over tables to get at each other. It's like war.

I saw all that, and I was leery of kids. I started coming to Cross Roads, still a little bit leery of kids, and God took it right out of my heart. He showed me there are good kids in this world. There are going to be more good kids in the world. I've seen thousands of them come through here. They're never the same when they leave here. And the good kids can help the kids that don't have the guidance. They're the ones who can change the world.

One thing that's special is that we don't have all the outside activities. It's put on the youth director, the counselors, the team to bond, to work out the differences between this group and that group, this person and that person. We don't even have soda water out here. We don't bring the world in. We bring the kids in from the world. And we watch God mold and shape them through their counselors, their team, their youth directors.

It's about inside activities, inside your heart. It's awesome to see youths sitting there praying, studying their Bible. To look out those kitchen windows and see them walking down to the worship area to pray, walking over to the Prayer Labyrinth.

Coming to me, they'll ask, "Are we able to walk on that labyrinth whenever we want?"

"That labyrinth is here for you to use."

They come to me and ask questions, and to answer those kids, you gotta be prayed up. You've got to know your Bible. You sure don't want to say something that isn't right. Lead them down the wrong path.

Being affiliated, I can go walk the Prayer Labyrinth anytime. Go sit in the chapel anytime. Go to the outside worship anytime. I live right down the road and I've got the keys.

My heart's desire is to be down here and serve God's people. I never dreamed I'd be here. I never dreamed I'd be doing anything like this.

The odds of us getting together were phenomenal. The boys and I went to the Methodist Church in town, and people were so friendly. I was still hiding, staying away from people, had been hurt, used and abused by people in the world. The next Sunday, we went to Sunday School, then to church. I met more of the women, and the boys got into the youth group. Then I met Hilda, and the boys started working out here.

Walking those trees with a chainsaw, God has always been in me, but I wasn't hearing Him. And if Cross Roads hadn't moved in a mile away, who knows where I would have been? If Cross Roads wasn't here, and I wasn't a part of it, I can't imagine.

Those who hope in the Lord will renew their strength. They will soar on wings like eagles; they will run and not grow weary, they will walk and not be faint. - Isaiah 40:31

CHAPTER 21

Soaring on Eagle's Wings

Those fall and winter months of 1999 were hard on all of us, but it was nice to finally have a fireplace to sit beside. No more shivering in front of a piece of bare plywood. Plus, an anonymous angel had left $1,000 cash in my mailbox, the exact amount I needed to patch my roof.

Another high point of that year came by way of my best friend, Mary. I was in the habit of dropping by the office where she worked and having lunch with her in their coffee bar. Those were bright spots in my day and special, I think, for both of us. We solved all the problems of the world over countless burgers, or salads, depending on whether one of us was dieting. One April morning Mary called me.

"Hey girl, you coming by for lunch today?"

"Maybe. I have an appointment that could take a while."

"Take your time, I'll wait. I have an idea I want to discuss with you."

No sooner had I sat down than Mary said, "You all need more help with Cross Roads."

"No, you really think so?" My sarcasm only made her smile.

"You know the Brazos Valley Emmaus Community holds four large retreats every year." Her blue eyes glowed with excitement. "They really need a more convenient and cost effective location for their events."

The Emmaus Walk I had attended was held at Camp Tejas in Giddings. I wouldn't have called it inconvenient, but I got her point. "You think they'd want to have their retreats at Cross Roads?"

"I think you should talk to them about signing a contract with Cross Roads."

During the next hour, as we batted around the possibilities, my enthusiasm mounted. *How would they feel about partnering with Cross Roads? What assurances would they need? What would we need? What timetable would they require?*

A contract would be the answer to everything. Perhaps other nearby Emmaus communities might be interested in contracting with Cross Roads, too. With guaranteed income, we could plan. We might even be able to get a loan.

That night I shared Mary's idea with Jennifer and Scott, who embraced it just as enthusiastically as I had. The next day Scott ran the idea by Jim Smith, our banker friend. We all agreed that the proposal to the Brazos Valley Emmaus Community (BVEC) needed to be made as strong as possible and as soon as possible. We'd only get one shot at it. Once again, we combined Scott's expertise in graphic design and marketing with my experience in making sales presentations. And once again, we hunkered down creating charts and graphs and compiling data.

A couple of months later, Scott and I apprehensively addressed the board with Scott's very professional PowerPoint presentation while Jennifer waited on a bench outside. The board members listened with rapt attention as we offered to tailor the camp facilities to meet their every need, since whatever footprint would work for them would work beautifully for any other retreat. The engineers in the group lit up as we suggested they help design the buildings and the placement of the structures. The treasurer scrutinized our proposed pricing.

A few heads cocked, and a couple nodded, when we asked for their long-term commitment. We were not asking for money, we were asking for partnership. We requested they put the word out to the community about the partnership to encourage members to help by donating or discounting their contracting services, or possibly by co-signing on a building loan.

Fifteen sets of eyes sparkled at the prospect set before them. The questions came at us fast and furious as the board prepared for a discussion of the possibilities. How long before the camp would be ready? How long was that price good for? How far was Cross Roads from West Houston? Champing at the bit to begin their discussion, they ushered us out of the room and asked us to wait.

Nervously optimistic, we filled Jennifer in on what had transpired, then we joined hands in prayer. It seemed like an hour before they called us back in for their verdict. With summer upon us and facing another season with the camp still unfinished, we scanned each face for a clue to what we were about to hear.

Chairman of the Board spoke four of my favorite words, "You've got a deal."

We flew out of there soaring on eagle's wings. Jennifer knew from the looks on our faces that the news was good. We made it to the parking lot before collapsing on each other in joyful tears of relief.

Cross Roads had a partner. There was light at the end of the tunnel.

A Summer Wedding

Summer was our off-season, the time we usually spent working on our houses and the camp facilities. But this year was different. Jennifer turned her loving attention to helping Tina plan her and Jeremy's wedding. Jennifer was in her social element and loving it. Also, it helped keep her mind off of the renovations on her house that were not getting done.

During high school, in Junior Achievement, Tina had discovered that she had a gift for accounting. Considering my financial status, and her family's attitude about the marriage, she realized she and Jeremy would have to pay for most of their wedding themselves. Fortunately, Jeremy was making good money at a company in Dallas, handling their technical and computer needs. Tina also had definite ideas about what she wanted in a wedding. After a ton of research poring over bridal magazines and calling various suppliers, she put together a budget that incorporated both her frugal nature and everything she'd dreamed that her wedding day should be.

The wedding party assembled on a blistering hot Texas day. Friends and family came from all over Texas. You could feel the peace and presence of the Holy Spirit in the gorgeous historical sanctuary. Soft light filtered through multi-colored stained glass windows, illuminating the wall of pipes, belonging to the grand organ, and Jeremy, beaming with joy and wonder as he anticipated his bride's arrival.

Jeremy, my second child and only son, was about to be married. I couldn't believe it. Tina, apprehensive that her father would show up and make a scene, nonetheless beamed as she was escorted down the aisle on the arm of her best friend. Carol had created beautiful presentations of fruit, vegetable, and cheese trays. Chafing dishes brimmed with steaming Swedish meatballs, and platters were stacked high with chicken salad sandwiches.

With the addition of punch, coffee, music, friends, and family, Jennifer and Tina had pulled together a recipe for a wonderful wedding.

As music emanated from the CD player in the church Fellowship Hall, Jeremy escorted his radiant bride onto the dance floor. I watched them embrace, and my thoughts turned to that traumatic day so long ago when I questioned God, screaming, "What have I done? Why is this happening? Why are You taking my son away?"

Now, as Jeremy and Tina moved seamlessly in unison to the music and gazed adoringly into each other's eyes, I realized that God had indeed known exactly what He was doing. He had answered my prayer by taking care of my son His way.

Above all, keep loving one another earnestly, since
love covers a multitude of sins. - 1 Peter 4:8

CHAPTER 22

There Are No Perfect People

While all of us were dancing and celebrating the bride and groom, my brother, John, a structural engineer, took me aside and mentioned that he'd noticed my house still needed finishing.

"You need a porch," he said, as we munched from the veggie tray together.

Concern showed in his eyes, as he reflected on the state of my house. No landing, no railing, just a shaky three-step ladder up to the front door.

"I have a brand new chimney," I pointed out. After barely scraping together the resources for the fireplace, buying the materials to replace the porch was not in the budget.

"We need to build you a porch," John said.

Was he serious? I hesitated to get into a conversation with my brother. John is known for stirring up situations that invariably lead to heated debates. But God had shown me, time and time again, that His way of taking care of me was through the people He sent my way. Was He sending my brother this time?

In our family of five siblings, I came first, with John arriving three years later. He was fifteen when my parents settled me at college and moved to Scotland. Separated, we grew apart during those formative childhood years and never quite regained a sense of closeness in adulthood.

I'm not sure what happened during those years in Scotland. I wasn't there.

But while in Scotland, John became completely disgusted with all things religious. Because of that, we tread lightly about discussing faith around him.

One day he told our sister, Sara, "You are going to let your Christianity drive a wedge between us."

"I'm not the one who's upset with me being a Christian," she said. "You're the one making an issue out of it, not me."

Although I don't talk about my faith with him, unless asked, John seems to be angry with me for making my relationship with God a priority.

"Who are you to be doing this?" he asked me, after hearing about Cross Roads. "You're divorced. A single parent. What makes you so special?"

"I'm just following a path I believe I'm intended to take."

"All Christians are hypocrites," he taunted.

"Yep, you're right. There are no perfect people."

So when John decided to build me a porch, I didn't know what to make of it. But this was my son's wedding day, and I was simply happy that everybody was getting along.

An Eye for Structure

A week or so after the wedding, John returned to Cross Roads and took umpteen meticulous measurements for the porch. I was blown away to see him following through on what he had proposed. He didn't ask for money to buy the materials, which was good, because I didn't have it. And a few weeks later, he returned with his perky, no non-sense daughter, Kati, and her doting boyfriend in tow.

Putting the porch together was quite a production. John had precut the boards and predrilled the holes for the screws. Amazingly, it went together like pieces of a finely crafted puzzle. Every board, every screw slipped exactly into place. We had it built in a day. I was elated.

I still didn't know how to reconcile John's generosity with all the times he had so outspokenly criticized me. I truly believe it was his way to show that, despite our differences, he still cared about me. Whatever the reason, I feel blessed every time I look at my perfect porch.

Struggles and Disconnections

Nina had a particularly difficult senior year at school. She was a good kid in most of the important ways. She didn't drink, smoke, or do drugs, but she was rebellious and very emotional, and we fought a lot.

That was also her boy-crazy year. Her boyfriend was two years older and had already graduated high school. She began skipping classes to hang out with him. After a number of absences the school would call me at work to ask why she was not in class, then I'd have to confront her when I got home. We fought about typical teen stuff, too, like making a mess in the house and not cleaning it up. But mostly we fought about my cell phone.

In those days, cell phones were brand new, clunky, and terribly expensive to use. The cellular company charged for every minute. I was now in outside sales at a commercial printing company, and as such I was issued a cell phone to keep in touch with the office, and the phone was paid for by the company.

If Nina couldn't find the peanut butter, she'd call me. If she heard the dog bark, she'd call me. Senseless phone calls, and every month my employer would caution me about the overages. Almost every night, Nina and I argued about it, but the next day she couldn't keep her antsy fingers from calling Mom.

"You don't understand, Nina. I'm going to lose my job, the job that feeds us. You can't phone me unless it's really important." I did not comprehend why she couldn't grasp that concept.

"Okay, I won't call! Even if the house is burning down. Or if I fall and break a leg … Or if I slice my finger off fixing lunch. I'll lie there bleeding in pain until you get home, but I won't call!"

The next day, she'd call to ask me some silly question. Finally, I told the printing company I'd pay the difference. I couldn't afford to pay it, and thankfully that never actually came about, but I was honestly afraid that I'd be fired.

Sweet and Challenging

Nina had always been a challenge. A beautiful baby, and sweet. But she failed to thrive, she couldn't keep food down, and she was hyper and irritable.

Twice she came down with pneumonia. The second time, our family doctor was out of town, with another doctor covering his patients. She couldn't examine my daughter with the stethoscope, because Nina was extremely ticklish and didn't like to be touched. She kicked, squirmed, wailed, and wouldn't stay on the bed. The doctor asked if I thought Nina might be hyperactive. I'd never heard of ADHD, so she gave me a book to read, *The Hyperactive Child* by Paul H. Wender, M.D. A lot of people today don't believe ADHD is real, but that book pegged Nina.

We did the psychological testing, the physical testing, the achievement testing, and the IQ testing. We got notes from her teacher. It took about two months to confirm the doctor's diagnosis. Nina began taking Ritalin, and within a year she had advanced two grades in school. After that, her life zoomed … until she entered high school.

"My friends don't like me when I take Ritalin," she complained.

When she became hyper and disruptive again, I realized she wasn't taking her medication. As a toddler, I could coax her into doing what was best for her. As a teenager, no amount of coaxing worked. All the disruptive agitation she'd shown in those early days returned, in the guise of acting out.

Looking back, I wonder if we might have escaped all the drama of those teen years had I been more insistent about her meds. She was approaching adulthood, and I believed she had a right to choose between the feelings she experienced of being subdued on Ritalin and the hyper behavior she expressed without it.

All in all, her senior year was one long struggle for both of us.

*... let us throw off everything that hinders and the sin
that so easily entangles, and let us run with perseverance
the race marked out for us.* - Hebrews 12:1

CHAPTER 23

Running in Place

Although we now had the security provided by the contract from Emmaus, the fall and winter months were again hard on all of us. Shortly after the wedding hoopla subsided, Jennifer and Scott, who had a second baby now on the way, decided they had no choice but to carve out time to build a safe yard for Grace to play in. They cleared the brush from a sizable area behind their house and enclosed the space with a pretty white picket fence.

Scott's dad and step mom brought out pallets of hardy Zoysia grass, which wouldn't need much mowing or water. We all pitched in to plant the grass, and Jennifer made flowerbeds, filling them with Gerbera daisies in vibrant colors. She couldn't expand their home to better accommodate their expanding family, but at least she could make it homey.

Scott, determined to build a new bathroom before fall, labored every evening after work and long into the night. After he'd started tearing out fixtures and replacing them, he couldn't just randomly stop. The bathroom had to remain usable as much as possible during the reconstruction, which meant timing it right and staying with it even when he was exhausted. Still, there were a few days when their little family was forced to trudge next door to use the bathroom at my house.

The fix-up was like sticking a wad of bubblegum on a leaky pipe, and we all knew it. That place would never be the home Jennifer and Scott wanted. With the nesting instinct taking over, Jennifer wanted a "real" house for their growing family.

I told them they could have some land to build on. Excited at the prospect, they started figuring out how to go about it financially. Scott, always creative, fantasized about the possibilities of an eco-friendly experimental house using solar panels for electricity, hay bales, or bottles for insulation, and maybe a windmill-generated water pump. He wanted hardwood floors. Jen wanted to raise their kids on carpet in a "normal" house built on a slab, so they could play and she could do aerobics without shaking the rafters.

But fall had arrived, along with the first campers of the new season. Their arrival brought a cheery reminder of why we were living out here in substandard conditions, working at jobs that barely paid our daily expenses then volunteering our weekends for manual labor and spiritual support to people we scarcely knew. Jennifer continually amazed me by coming up with innovative programs for our visitors. Scott mowed the grass, ran the weed whacker, and performed countless other necessary tasks. Carol turned out breakfast, lunch, and dinner fare that sparked hungry smiles at mealtimes. And all of us pitched in to do the dishes, sweep and mop the cabins, take out the trash, clean the showers, and scour the toilets.

Amazingly, those busy weekends were still the best part of our year.

The Company of Others

Watching the many different ways people choose to worship was an eye-opening experience. From the beginning, Cross Roads was receptive to any religious organization, regardless of their creed, and I've wondered over the years if one reason God chose me for this work was because my personal doctrine encouraged me to be open and accepting of everyone. As first a Presbyterian, second a Methodist, and then non-denominational, I viewed most people who worshipped God in a manner different from mine as "interesting" rather than "wrong." But I hadn't considered the wide assortment of devout followers who would eventually be drawn to the camp.

Possibly one of the most interesting groups was the Buddhists. A yoga institute from Houston sent their advisors ahead to check us out thoroughly, because they were bringing in lineage masters from Korea. The scouts reported back to their committee. They were fully aware of our minimal facilities before booking their event. But when the leader arrived, who had not been among the scouts, she was appalled.

"Where are the Masters going to sleep? Where will they eat?"

Apparently, it wouldn't do to have these holy men mixing so intimately with their local Buddhist community. In the end, they were given a separate cabin for sleeping, and small tables were placed out in the woods so they could eat privately. Women wearing white pajama-like tops and pants bowed and scraped as they carried food to them.

Anyone who knows me knows that I found these practices difficult to watch. Concealing my discomfort and showering them with Christ's love was a challenge. I failed. It was the only time Carol suggested that I just go home and let her handle things. I think perhaps God was opening my eyes once more to the fact that Cross Roads was His camp, not mine and He'd bring whoever

He wanted to the camp. Our job was to love them on His behalf. He dropped lots of surprises on us.

Ferdinand Finds a Home

One day a bull showed up in our yard. Because we're surrounded by ranches and farms, we just chuckled and started calling our neighbors to find out whose fence was down. After exhausting our list, and receiving no calls on the flyers we posted, we still hadn't located the bull's home. No one seemed to be missing the animal.

"Then it must be mine," Scott said, grinning broadly. "God knows I always wanted to raise cattle."

As a boy, Scott often visited his grandfather in the country and enjoyed helping with the animals. When he asked for his own cow, his grandfather bought him one. Cross Roads reminded Scott of those childhood visits with his grandfather, and while he hadn't talked about it much, I knew he hoped to eventually run a few cattle on our 160 acres.

Having a bull show up on his doorstep was all the encouragement Scott needed. He named the bull Ferdinand, and a short time later he brought home a heifer.

Despite our recent partnership agreement with Emmaus, and the progress we'd made on our homes during the summer, we still had a lot of concerns weighing on us. Nina and I were at odds. Jennifer was pregnant, with Grace barely a toddler, so her hands were more than full. Scott stayed busy constantly. We needed a pick-me-up, and Ferdinand gave that to us. By spring, Cross Roads had a bull calf.

Not long afterward, Ferdinand must have decided Cross Roads wasn't fun anymore, and he just disappeared. But he left his mark: we now had a heifer and a calf that came bellowing across the yard every time we unloaded groceries from the car. They thought the rustling grocery bags were feed sacks and would push, pull, and fight us for the bags all the way up the steps.

Partners

Our partnership with Emmaus boosted our morale, because the BVEC provided credibility we hadn't yet gained on our own. Our contract specified they would hold their biannual retreats at Cross Roads. Scott, Jennifer, and I speculated that if we could arrange similar contracts with other Emmaus communities, we could take the package to the bank for collateral against a loan.

Even though every penny earned from retreats was turned right back into supplies, materials, building and maintenance, with no one being paid for the hours we worked, the camp facilities were a long way from complete. A loan was still the best way to make that happen a little faster. Meanwhile, we continued taking baby steps.

Campers knew that their fees were used to improve the camp, and they liked that. Each time they returned, they delighted at seeing a specific improvement, such as new benches or a new element for the obstacle course, which their money had helped provide.

That meant we had to *spend* money, we couldn't hoard it. We had to constantly be doing something to show our faith in the venture; otherwise, people who believed in us would lose confidence. On the whole, people tend to think, "If *you're* scared, then why should I support you?"

We baby-stepped a fine line that winter, spending and doing enough to show progress without depleting our skimpy funds. Scott and Jennifer continued designing their dream home on paper. Then, as winter approached, we learned that sometimes God's blessing comes disguised as bad news.

The bank officer shifted uneasily in his big chair as he spoke.

"Ma'am, all those hundred and sixty acres are collateral against the loan. You can't just give some to your kids."

"What about paying down the loan?"

"Hmmm, let me look at something." He scrolled through our records on his computer, which faced away from me. "No, I can't do that without your ex-husband's approval."

"What?" That would never happen. "That's impossible. Why?"

He explained that while I owned the land, the bank had made the loan to both of us, and Steve was still a co-signer on the note. I would have to apply for a new loan, for which I knew I could not qualify.

A Brief Insanity

Shaken to the core, I felt that I was about to fail God and everyone who had put their faith in Cross Roads. Without a decent house to live in, Jennifer and Scott would be compelled to move away, sooner rather than later. Nina, graduating in May, planned to move away to college. I might even lose the land God had entrusted to me.

I spent many sleepless nights tearfully pleading, "God, what is your plan? How am I supposed to do this?"

That sense of impending failure, ignited abandonment issues that had lain dormant since my family's move to Scotland when I was a teen. Psychologists say that when you are in crisis, you revert to what you know, so to make matters worse, I let another man into my life. And Nina went ballistic.

It was a four-month whirlwind. This man had recently moved to town to take a job as the elementary school's new principal. In a short time, he cultivated an aura of respectability by joining the church and several community organizations. We courted briefly and married just before Christmas.

Nina despised and distrusted him. In near hysteria, she refused to attend the wedding, but finally appeared at the church with her boyfriend and sat in a back pew, crying.

New Year's Eve arrived and, as was our custom, we lit fireworks to celebrate every blessing of the previous year and those God had in store for us in the year ahead. A few weeks later my new husband, after looking over my paltry financial statement, walked out, leaving me humiliated.

The divorce should have been a mere formality. I almost didn't hire a lawyer, but thank God Jennifer insisted that I at least have someone read over the papers. The attorney discovered a bizarre clause had been inserted that would have given this man the right to go back to court without notifying me and claim all of my property. He wore out his welcome rapidly in Caldwell and by summer had left town for good. I learned later that I wasn't his first victim.

Long before the ink was dry on my divorce papers, I had spun into a deep depression. I felt that I'd lost my mind and any credibility that I, or my ministry, may have gained over the years. Mary sat with me in a city park, praying while I sobbed my heart out. I remember fearing that if she didn't hold me tight enough I would fly apart.

Fortunately, I'm blessed to be surrounded by good friends who helped me through a period, which I would like to rip from my calendar and burn. Girlfriends from my Accountability Group counseled and prayed with me. Jennifer, Scott, and Carol cried and prayed. My sister, Sara, heard about my problems and, worried, came up from Clear Lake to console me. Christ used friends and family to literally save my life.

But the final blow of that grievous winter had not yet hit. A new board had taken office at the BVEC, and we learned that this new board was rescinding the previous board's agreement with Cross Roads.

REFLECTIONS

When belief systems fail, it is often because people have put their faith in formulas, rituals, denominations, traditions, actions, intellect or other people instead of simply seeking a personal relationship with Christ and a deep understanding of His will for their lives. His will for us is much more than a code of conduct or a set of rules to be used to restrict our creativity or intellect.

We humans have powerful spiritual hungers. The many religions on our planet are all efforts to meet these spiritual needs. Religion can be either a set of wings for our souls or a lead weight around our necks.

God was known in different ways by different people whose experiences of Him were varied. Abraham, Isaac, Jacob and Moses all worshiped the same God, but each called Him by a different name according to their experience of Him. I am known as Hilda, Mom, Sister, Aunt, Daughter, Honey, each name describing the nature of the relationship each person has with me. The different names the ancients had for God tell us about their personal relationship with God, and their witness revealed new characteristics of God's nature for all of us.

When we open our minds and meditate or pray, we are open to that power that is the power of the Holy Spirit, and in so doing we allow that power to use us, fill us, happen to us. Many individuals never experience that power, and that is just sad. Children are typically open, willing and eager, and it is my calling to provide a safe place for young seekers to satisfy their spiritual hungers in a profound and personal interaction with Christ. Cross Roads is that place.

Hilda Hellums Baker, 2004

And this is the confidence that we have toward Him, that if we ask anything according to His will He hears us .-1 John 5:14-15

CHAPTER 24

Millennium Year

The year of 2000 passed in a blur, as if the Emmaus reversal had knocked our vision out of kilter. With our hopes of getting a loan quashed for the second and final time, we needed to find alternate means of raising serious money. But where did we start looking?

At work, my cubicle sat not far from the office manager's desk. Speaking low enough on the phone to prevent being heard by other office personnel was practically impossible, and the office manager, Melissa Dunn, called me aside one day.

"What's this camp I hear you talking about?"

Uh-oh. Caught. I tried not to discuss my private business on company time.

"Sometimes I have to take the calls," I said, "There is a lot happening out there."

"No, really, tell me about it," Melissa said, smiling. "What kind of camp are you running out there in Chriesman?"

A private person with the jaw set of a pit bull, Melissa was a "thirty-something" no non-sense single businesswoman. We went to lunch, and I told her about Cross Roads. After that, she asked me almost daily for an update on how things were going with the camp. She took the opportunity, upon hearing about the challenge we had undertaken, to apply her formidable detective abilities. One day she pulled me aside again.

"I heard about a nursing home that's being demolished. It's full of furniture, kitchen equipment, beds, everything. You could use some of that stuff when you build your kitchen and the new cabins."

"Well, sure we could."

"They're not planning to sell the stuff, just bulldozing it along with building. Why don't we call and see if we can get it?"

"Okay. But I don't know where we'd store it."

"We can worry about that later."

The nursing home agreed that we could take anything we needed. Before I knew it, Melissa had found a company in Oklahoma willing to donate a forty-foot storage trailer. A few days later, a man drove down from American Freightways in a tractor-trailer rig and unhooked his entire trailer unit, wheels and all, outside Scott and Jennifer's house. God seemed to be paving the way once again, this time through my tenacious new friend.

Scott, with the help of Jim Smith, organized a work detail to take apart the nursing home. For three weekends in a row during that hot summer, we salvaged lighting fixtures, wall switches, towel dispensers, tables, chairs, a stove and a stainless steel table from the kitchen, wall hangings, and shelves. Nailed down or not, if it was salvageable, we grabbed it.

If I learned anything that summer, it was that Melissa Dunn truly is a bulldog. When she gets hold of something, she won't let it go. God knew that Melissa was exactly the person we needed to kick us back into action and make us change gears.

With the Emmaus contract gone, and no possibility of borrowing money, we needed a new strategy. We needed cash more than anything, but if we could scavenge building materials, or get them donated, then we could surely round up volunteer work crews.

Scott is a natural scavenger. Soon the storage trailer was overflowing onto the yard and under tarps. He got a friend of his to donate a walk-in freezer. All Scott had to do was to dismantle and move it. The dismantling process took a while.

"This will be great for our kitchen," he announced, when he brought it home, and stored it with the other great finds littering our yard.

"This place is beginning to look like a junkyard," Jennifer moaned.

I had to agree. But at least we were doing something to stay alive, to build for the future. People could see it, and a lot of them showed up to help us. We were hopeful.

Mission Trip Rescue

Like most Americans, I've watched "makeover" shows on TV and thought, "Wow, look at what a dismal mess that person or family had before, and look how fabulous it is now."

"It" might be anything from a personal wardrobe to an entire new home. But it wasn't until an anonymous Good Samaritan gave our name to an outreach program looking for potential work sites in our area that I realized how embarrassing a makeover might be to the person receiving it. Specifically, Jennifer's house became their mission field.

Every summer this organization gathers kids from all over Central Texas to band together and tackle projects. Someone had turned in Jennifer's house as a work site, and when they called, Scott's response was immediate, "Absolutely! I can use all the help I can get!"

Yes, the house needed work, a lot of work. And yes, our Good Samaritan had his (or her) heart in the right place. And yes, the kids were amazing in their selfless attack on the crooked little cottage that had been sawed in half the wrong way by Dumb 'n' Dumber and nailed back together without the benefit of professional levelers, roofers, plumbers, or electricians. But Jennifer was appalled. Having traveled with her own youth group on many similar missions, she was accustomed to being on the "other side of the crumbling walls."

At home with Grace that year, Jennifer just couldn't handle it. After the first day she packed Grace up and spent the next two days in town.

For their part, the kids were energetic and tireless. They discovered the attic was full of wasp's nests. In removing them, some of the kids got stung. But they persevered and bravely removed every wasp. Then they scraped, patched, and painted the house. They were tremendously proud of their achievement.

But the truth is, the walls were thin and Jennifer, from inside her bedroom, had heard their comments as they assessed the project.

"How can she live here?" said one.

"I'd just burn it," said another.

Jennifer found it demeaning and felt the kids were judging her. She didn't need that, so she left.

Seeing Through the Blur

Looking back, I see the millennium year as a mixture of good things that happened and things that were not so good. In some ways, it seems like a year of wasted energy.

But Jennifer's pregnancy, while not easy, progressed without any big problems. Clayton was born in April, a perfect boy to finish out their perfect little family.

Nina was the trainer on the girls' basketball team. She also worked the camera for them, and it was the first year Nina had really felt a part of something at that school. It should have been a lot of fun for both of us.

Project Graduation kicked off, and in a small-town high school, that's a big deal. When the committee asked me to help, I declined, not realizing that parents were "expected" to participate. Emotionally, physically, monetarily, I didn't have the wherewithal to do it. I was just running in place trying to keep up with life and getting farther and farther behind. Later, I realized how much I had disappointed my daughter, in so many ways and on so many levels. It would have been better for Nina if I'd gotten more involved in her life. She went to the prom with her boyfriend and life would never be the same for her again.

Blessed is the one who finds wisdom, and the one who gets understanding, for the gain from her is better than gain from silver and her profit better than gold. - Proverbs 3:13-17

CHAPTER 25

Horses for Christmas

With that difficult senior year behind her, Nina relocated to Bryan to start college at Blinn. The apartment locators matched her with three roommates who were already friends and who loved to drink and party, not a good fit at all for Nina, who continued to walk the straight and narrow when it came to alcohol, drugs, or smoking. She also discovered that, unless she locked her door before she went out, her roommates would go in and mess with her belongings.

One Foot in Front of the Other

In the movie *What About Bob?* Bill Murray as Bob Wiley has been told by his therapist that he can do anything he wants if he takes it in baby steps. That is absolutely my favorite movie.

Throughout the film, Bob is murmuring, "… baby steps … baby steps … baby step to the elevator … baby step *into* the elevator …"

At Cross Roads, we found ourselves so many days just putting one foot in front of the other, moving resolutely toward whichever current goal we'd set for ourselves. Occasionally, I found myself muttering, just like Bob. "Baby steps, baby steps. Baby-steps to improve our houses … baby-step to enclose the pavilion …."

As I looked back at the previous year, I couldn't help wondering if God was using the perpetual setbacks that kept shutting me down to teach me not to move so fast. Maybe He was saying to me, "Slow down, pay attention, *what about Me?*"

Over the years, opportunities for various Bible Studies seemed to present themselves at amazingly appropriate times. These studies were a crucial part of my faith journey. After all, I reasoned, anything you want to do well requires study and practice. You can't play an instrument without lessons, or baseball if you don't know the rules. Most worthwhile endeavors require time, study and practice, learning to live your faith is no different. Studies like "Experiencing God" by Henry T. Blackaby & Claude V. King, "Purpose Driven Life" by Rick Warren, and "Anchoring Your Well Being" by Howard Clinebell, Ph.D., among others, proved to be life preservers in my wave-tossed life and each provided critical tools as I searched for my direction and the direction for the camp. Much of my personal healing also took place in the intimacy of these small group studies. Quickly, I recognized these offerings as chances to prepare for future trials that only God knew lay in my path.

And while we were up to our ears in other problems at Cross Roads, the campers never ceased to be a blessing. I've been a speaker on several women's retreats held at other camps, and every time God would send at least one person that I felt a strong connection to. One weekend, after I spoke to a women's group about being a single mom and starting the camp, a lady came over to me.

"I want you to know you answered an important question for me," she said.

"Really?" A statement like that is always a little scary.

"I'm a single mom, too. I have a daughter. And I've wanted to go into the ministry. I believe that's what I'm supposed to do. Now, after this weekend and hearing your story, I have the courage to do it."

Today that woman is an ordained minister. What I learned from her is that God is going to use me, and Cross Roads, for more than just what happens at the camp. It's bigger than that. He's bigger than that. As I put one foot in front of the other, He is showing me that Cross Roads is about stepping out in faith, trusting the Lord. He was using Bible studies, friends, retreats, and even every difficulty to prepare me, and to heal me. Healing, I was learning, is not a one-shot deal. Growth is seldom easy, and it's not always in the direction we expect. And one by one He was continuing to pry my fingers off the control stick of His mission for me.

Stand at the Crossroads

One thing I do, when I'm really struggling to understand, is flip through my Bible until a word or a sentence stands out. Invariably, it will speak to me. My battered Bible looks like a kid took markers to it. My devotional books are the same.

On countless occasions, through scripture, God says, "I'm there for you, just open your eyes."

Early on, when we had to send the realtor our offer for this property, we didn't have letterhead, so Scott threw something together. We hadn't even named the retreat we envisioned. We weren't yet real. I went to the Bible, and on the third page I flipped to, this verse appeared:

> *Stand at the crossroads and look; ask for the ancient paths, ask where the good way is, and walk in it, and you will find rest for your souls ...*
>
> - Jeremiah 6:16 (NIV)

Where was I standing but at a crossroads? I showed the passage to Scott and Jennifer, and Cross Roads instantly became our name. It's amazing to me the way the Spirit works.

My way of talking to God might be considered unusual by some. Many people sit down or kneel quietly at specific times and pray. Unfortunately, I don't usually make time to do that. I just talk to Him all day long, as I would to anyone. It's not "normal" prayer in the way that prayer is generally viewed. Breath Prayers, repeating prayers that can be said in a single breath like *God be my strength,* as I inhale, and as I exhale saying *today and every day*, also help keep my focus on Him continuously.

It's a relationship, as if God is sitting in a chair across from me, walking beside me, or joining me in a self-indulgent, calorie-laden heaping dish of Bluebell Rocky Road ice cream. Occasionally, I do sit quietly and pray, often I groan and fuss. But mostly we just talk.

Seated: Dr. Jean Bailey, Ph.D., Jane Pulley, and Ellen Knight.
Standing: Hilda Hellums & Cindy VanDeventer

Accountability

From very early in this venture, Cindy VanDeventer was instrumental in helping me find my way. Her considerable contribution to the camp was the way in which she promoted me and Cross Roads to the community. She talked about it constantly to everyone she knew, everyone she met, talking it up. She was my advocate to groups, to churches, to people in Caldwell and Bryan. She was so proud of what we were doing that her contagious enthusiasm spread to other people like wildfire.

Cindy supported me personally, making sure I attended that Walk to Emmaus. She hosted a Bible study in her home. She found resources for me, spiritual resources, and insisted I take time for them. She told me where opportunities were happening.

One of the many ways she influenced my journey was by inviting me to join her Accountability Group, which has proved a continuous source of spiritual growth and support. It's all women, and as I write this, I've been in this group for twelve years, meeting every Thursday at noon in College Station. Cindy was one of the originators. Women have come and gone, but the group has been there for me during good times and bad. When I thought I was losing my mind, or I was physically hurt, or I had financial disasters, or any kind of problem, they were there not only to talk me through it but also to lend their wholehearted assistance.

We take care of each other. More importantly, we hold each other accountable to our relationship with Christ and with ourselves. We ask questions every week. "When did you feel closest to Christ this week?" Or, "Where did you see Him at work in your life?"

Talking it out makes us intensely aware of where God is present in our lives, because we know we'll have to answer questions about our experiences the following week.

"What was your call to discipleship? Were you called to do anything extraordinary? Or to help another person?"

"Did your church ask you for assistance? Did you have to counsel a person who was having a difficult day?"

Or, "When did you deny your discipleship? When did you not live your Christian principles? What did you do about that?"

We don't get to slide. We have to answer to ourselves, to the group, and most importantly, to Christ.

My Accountability Group, that collection of incredible women, more than any other one element, has been the key to my hanging in when I felt down and discouraged. These women kept me focused on the mission. They kept me accountable. They kept me sane.

Accountability came strongly into focus in November of that millennium year. I hadn't seen Nina since she left for college in August, but she and my best friend Mary had gotten close. So when

I stopped off at Mary's office for lunch one day, Nina was there. She looked fantastic, and I took the opportunity to tell her so.

"Nina, you look really good. You've put on a little weight, your complexion is glowing. You look fabulous."

The next day, moments before going in to the morning sales meeting, I got an email from her. "Well, I guess you figured it out. I'm pregnant."

No, that possibility had never entered my mind, but I thanked God that it was a Thursday and my Accountability Group would be meeting. Seven months had passed since the night of Nina's senior prom. Now she was seven months pregnant and scared to death. Finishing college, getting her degree, was important to Nina, and she wanted to stay at school and continue. I told her this pregnancy meant she'd have to put her education on hold. I knew of no way to pay for the upcoming childcare needed to continue school.

Two weeks later, she left school and came home.

Bah! Humbug!

I don't like holidays. As a single parent, holidays often meant sending my kids to visit their father and, especially during the years when my parents weren't speaking to me, sitting at home alone.

At Cross Roads, a holiday was treated as another workday, except for attending church. After Grace and Clayton were born, Scott and Jennifer usually went to Dallas or Houston to enjoy holiday weekends with one of Scott's parents. I understood this completely; after all, they lived with me most of the year, but with Jeremy gone, and Nina going to her dad's house every other holiday, that frequently left me on my own.

One morning close to Christmas, Scott came walking up the driveway leading a pair of horses. He knew I loved riding and that

I missed it. Being in the country, I couldn't help wanting another horse, but acquiring one had never been in our budget. To keep and care for a horse properly, you need things we didn't have, a fenced pasture or barn, for example. You also need a saddle and other tack, grooming implements, feed and buckets.

But seeing those horses amble up the path behind my son-in-law, I was thrilled. We all ran out to meet them.

"You and Jennifer need leisure time and a special activity you can enjoy together," Scott explained.

I looked at Jennifer, who obviously felt as surprised as I did.

"Jennifer wants to learn to ride," Scott added. "And you can teach her."

For many people, the millennium was the year of Y2K, when the whole world freaked out about whether their computers would go bonkers. For us, the year 2000 was about disappointments, disillusionment, unending work, and a gorgeous pair of horses for Christmas.

I didn't want to move to Caldwell and leave my friends and everything I knew. From day one until the day I moved away years later, I felt like an outsider. Not having real friendships was the hardest. I had friends, but no female friends.

Mom gave all she had to the camp. She didn't have much left for me, and I needed her. Cross Roads was all I had, it was what I lived for, it gave me purpose and meaning. Cross Roads filled the voids I had in my life.

Cross Roads was gonna happen, and I never thought it wouldn't. Mom seemed to handle every obstacle like it was just that ... an obstacle we would get past to carry on with God's vision. She made it seem like there was so little to worry about.

Being at Cross Roads, I felt like I was contributing to a higher cause, making a place for people to come and experience God in profound ways. There is nothing better than doing God's work. There is nothing better for the soul than living God's work every day.

Our previous mission trips were always profound experiences. No matter where we went, we could feel God there, and I always looked forward to camps and trips. Louisiana and Tennessee were the best, where we were fixing up houses, scraping and painting. Those mission trips taught me the attitude of a servant's heart.

Cross Roads was a lifelong mission trip. I thought of it as an adventure. It was surreal ... but I knew people all over the county, people I went to school with, who had less than we did or had worse living conditions, so I never felt bad for myself. I knew it wasn't about the stuff or the house. I honestly could move back into Jennifer's old house, spruce it up, and be totally content. I love that house. It feels like home to me.

I loved helping build the maze, helping construct the first two cabins, helping build Noah's Ark. Helping Scott. Scott must have caught himself on fire ten times or more. I really clung to Scott during that time, because he was always there for me. No matter what awkward or hurtful thoughts I had, if I came to him with the right attitude, he was willing to talk with me, and not judge or condemn me or make me feel bad. Most of the time it was my own stupidity and pride that kept me from going to him, or to anyone.

The best time of my life was helping with the campers. My title was, "Youth Advisor," and I took my position very seriously. I was able to give insight on what youths would be excited about, what they would be bored with or turned away by. Being able to connect with the groups that came, to pour into their lives and to be poured into as well, was the greatest. I never walked away from a weekend without feeling more loved by God.

Retreats are essential to any youth ministry, big or small. To be able to get away from life, to build your group stronger and closer, and to experience God in ways you simply cannot do back home is absolutely essential. It is not just important, or something to strive towards, it's essential.

Life has trauma, no matter what your surroundings are. Jesus himself went through trials. To think I would escape life without trials would be totally ridiculous. The family issues would have followed us no matter where we lived. Cross Roads gave me a place to be at peace and feel the presence of God. When I was in deep need of feeling close to Him, I would drive or walk down to the camp and just pray. I really felt close to Him there.

It is my honor to say I was involved in helping God's vision come to life. I am honored to know that everything we did during those years gives people a place to come to, to reach God in ways they can't do 'back home'.

And the whole multitude sought to touch Him, for power
went out from Him and healed them all. -Luke 6:19

CHAPTER 26

Let Me Do It Myself!

Nina was terrified. At the age of nineteen, she had no idea how she was going to take care of a baby on her own. I didn't either. I remembered how hard it was when I became a single mom, and I was twenty-two at the time. I promised to help Nina all I could, and Paige was born perfect and sweet to a delighted mom and grand mom.

But if Nina was difficult to deal with under normal circumstances, Hormonal Nina was impossible. We argued daily.

Then on March 25, 2001, I broke my back.

The air outdoors was nippy, and it was easy to tell that Shadow, my white gelding, was feeling his oats. We'd had a great weekend with the youth from a church in College Station. The kids were already gone. Several of the counselors stayed behind to help the leaders, tie up loose ends, clean, and pack up their program materials. Scott was at the camp helping, too. I decided to ride my horse down to say goodbye and collect their check. It would be my first stop on a nice afternoon trail ride.

Shadow wasn't so sure he wanted to go. As I walked up to him with a feed bucket and halter, he stood with his back to me, observing me warily over his shoulder. Shaking his head, he tossed his black mane and tail from side to side as if to say, "Do you really want to do this?"

As I was about to put the rope over his neck, Shadow gave a little a jump and sprinted about fifty feet away. He liked to play hard to get. The feed bucket finally won him over and off we went. He pranced and sidestepped all the way down the road.

While Shadow usually loved attention, he was not himself that day. He didn't like it when the remaining campers gathered around to pet and admire him. He jerked his head away and shied to the side to avoid them. Resolving that caution is the highest form of valor, I decided to ride him back home and cancel my plans for a longer ride that afternoon.

Remounting was difficult. Shadow wouldn't stand still. One of the campers offered to hold him for me, but that didn't help.

"Let go," I said," let me do it myself."

As I pulled up, swinging my leg halfway over his hindquarters, he started bucking. For three jumps, I clung to the saddle horn, one foot in the stirrup, and kept trying to hoist the other leg over him. Then he leaped, twisted and lunged all at once, launching me backwards.

I landed with a sickening thud, first on my right hip, then my right shoulder. The back of my head crashed to the ground.

Intense pain prevented me from rolling over to get up, so I tried to just sit up, but froze in agony, with my head and legs off the ground and my knees flexed. I could neither sit up, nor lie back down.

Scott ran over to me, and upon realizing how bad it was, held my head on his knees. Someone else supported my legs while someone raced to the house for Jennifer.

She sped down the drive, threw on the brakes, and jumped out.

"Are you okay?"

"No. Call an ambulance."

The color drained from her face. She knew that if I said I needed help, it must be bad. She ran to the phone in the shed knowing full well that it rarely worked. The line was dead.

Later, she told me, "I slammed that phone down and prayed, 'God, I need this phone to work and I know you can do it.'" Absolutely confident it would work now... she picked it up and without listening for a dial tone, dialed 911. The call went through.

Lightning Bolts and Angels

The most infinitesimal movement, even a deep breath, sent lightning bolts of pain through my back. It hurt too much to cry. Several county EMTs arrived, but there was little they could do for what appeared to be a back injury. I continued to balance suspended between lying down and sitting up. My muscles burned from the effort of maintaining that exact position, even with the help from my new best friends.

I began the breathing exercise I'd learned twenty years before in Lamaze childbirth classes. This time I focused on an imaginary cross and chanted, "Please, help me Jesus," over and over again, and through the screeching pain, I felt His presence.

Breathe in, blow out, focus, focus ...

Incredibly, the pain diminished.

Each time a person spoke to me and my concentration was broken, the pain rushed back. I knew the EMTs were only doing their job with their poking and prodding, but finally, I lost my temper.

"You're killing me," I said, each word wracking me with pain. "Quit talking to me!"

After an interminable wait, which I'm sure wasn't nearly as long as it seemed, the ambulance arrived. Unlike in the movies, the EMTs were not authorized to start an IV, or give me anything effective for the pain. They lifted me onto a backboard and into the ambulance, an agonizing experience in itself. The ambulance ride was unbearable.

The driver was required to drive the speed limit because, while excruciating, my injury was not life threatening. During the ride one of the EMTs, I believe his nickname was Chicken, straddled me and lifted me by the small of the back to relieve some of the pain. His arms, back and legs, on fire from the strain, finally gave out, and I could read the dejection in his eyes.

"I'm sorry ma'am, I just can't do it anymore."

Unsure that my heart could take the level of pain I was experiencing for much longer, I prayed for unconsciousness. I stayed wide wake.

At the hospital, the nightmare continued. Nurses in the Emergency Room insisted that I lie still and flat, for my own good, but it was impossible, since they refused to give me anything effective for the pain. In radiology after several painful attempts to turn me on my side for X-rays they discovered my feet were still taped to the backboard I'd been brought in on.

Jennifer had followed me in, and she yelled at everyone in sight until someone finally tracked down an anesthesiologist. He came to the hospital, and the pain finally stopped. Relaxed and still, I slid deeper and deeper into myself.

To Dream Perchance to Heal

I woke from that blessed purple haze to a doctor standing by the bed. He was saying something, but his words jumbled in my head. Straining to make sense I got the gist of it, "... a compression fracture ... L3 lumbar ... crushed ... no surgical remedy. "But his last words pierced my heart. "Too soon to tell whether it will pinch off the nerves in your spinal cord."

If he said anything else, I didn't hear it. Slipping back into the void, I began to pray that I would be able to walk again.

Jennifer slept on a pallet by my hospital bed most nights, leaving Scott to take care of Grace and Clayton. Scott came by during the day. Nina, left on her own to care for her two-month-old daughter, was frantic because she had no one to keep Paige so that she could get to the hospital to see me.

Melissa Dunn spent hours sitting by my bed, guarding me, as I dozed in and out of a drug-induced sleep. Mary came to check daily. I was surrounded by love. On one of my pastor's visits, he stuck his head in the door, but quickly bowed out when he saw my bed ringed with women holding hands and praying over me.

There was no treatment, other than bed rest, pain meds, muscle relaxers, and a back brace. Over the next couple of weeks, I was weaned from the IV pain pump. Sitting, propped up in bed, was still extremely painful. Weak and shaky, I could not take more than a few steps at a time, even with a walker. As soon as I could make it to the bathroom and back using a walker, the hospital released me.

With the agonizing ambulance ride fresh in my memory, I dreaded the forty-five-minute drive home sitting upright in a bumpy car. I was thrilled when Angelique Gammon offered to drive me home in her comfy van. She and her husband, Greg, were friends from church as well as part owners of the printing company where I worked.

Jennifer arrived to take me home. Gingerly, I lowered myself into the wheel chair for the ride out to the pick-up zone where Angelique was waiting.

The first leg of the journey was all stops and starts along the city streets. The stabbing pains eased up a bit during the thirty minutes or so on the highway, only to begin again as we turned on to our rough county road. But the half-mile washboard incline to my house was the worst. It was all I could do not to scream.

When the van bounced to a stop, I stared dismally at the four steps up to the porch. Collecting my nerve, braced for pain, and with Jennifer and Angelique's help, I eased down from the van. Nina and Paige came banging through the screen door to greet me. Still supported on either side by Angelique and Jennifer, I maneuvered up the front steps one baby step at a time.

A New Friend

So, there we were. Nina, holed up in the back bedroom, her post partum hormones still raging and overwhelmed with the care of two-month-old Paige, while I was laid out, semi-conscious, in the front bedroom. My only TV was in the living room, too far to see or hear, and the pain meds kept me from focusing enough to read. I lay there day in and day out, drifting in and out, bored out of my mind.

I could hear my daughter struggling with her colicky baby, and it broke my heart not to be able to keep my promise to help. Nina checked on me periodically, but she had her hands full with Paige.

My bedroom window was at the front of the house, opening onto the wide shaded porch. Lying on my bed, I spent my days gazing down the long driveway waiting for Jennifer or Scott to come home, or for dinner to be delivered.

Obsessing over my helplessness, I began focusing on the cobwebs collecting in the corners of my room. I started bugging Jennifer about knocking them down. Patiently humoring me, she promised to clean them out as soon as she had time.

Time, a funny thought. I had all the time in the world and couldn't do anything. She, on the other hand, had a fulltime job, two small children, a hormonal nineteen-year-old sister with a newborn, a cranky mother with a broken back and a camp to take care of. And, God forgive me, I was annoyed about cobwebs.

Friends turned out in force, bringing food and sending tons of cards, all vowing to keep me in their prayers. Those thoughtful expressions of care were a source of reassurance that I needed badly, especially since by that time, I was pretty certain everybody in Caldwell was done with me, and my follies.

One day a high school friend of Nina's dropped by. Nina was a good listener, and Russel needed to talk. They spent the afternoon sitting on the porch swing. That night, he pitched in to help Nina with dinner. After we ate, he picked a hymnal out of the bookcase. Apparently, he'd been playing the piano in his church for years and was somewhat of a child prodigy. Sitting down at an ancient upright piano that had been donated to the camp, he began playing hymns. He continued entertaining us for over an hour, ending with a beautiful piece entitled "Walk In the Clouds," which he wrote himself. Then sheepishly, he told me he couldn't go home and asked if he could sleep on the couch for the night.

Still confined to bed, for the most part, I felt my heart quicken at the sound of the piano bench scooting into position each night. I lay listening from the adjoining room as he played hymn after hymn. The reassuring words and healing music soothed my mind and restored my soul. Russel continued sleeping on our couch for over a month before leaving to join the Air Force. I often thank God for dropping Russel into my life to speed my healing.

The drive to College Station and back for weekly doctor's appointments became increasingly bearable. At my two-month check up, the doctor slapped a new X-ray onto the lighted glass and pointed to an area on my spine.

"See this? That's your L3 vertebra. The one that was smashed."

Squashed short, opaque, and mottled, it differed from the other vertebrae like a raisin differs from a grape. It clearly had been pulverized and had re-solidified into a new shape. He then pointed to a slender thread just above it.

"That's the nerve. The bone hardened leaving barely enough space for your nerve to poke through. You are going to be fine."

I just silently smiled. While I was still at the camp, lying in pain on the ground and deeply focused in prayer, He and His angels had come to me. His hands touched me, and I experienced an overwhelmingly powerful and calming presence. I knew back then that everything would be okay.

Seeing that smashed vertebra on the X-ray only confirmed what I already knew.

When you believe that nothing significant can happen through you, you have said more about your belief in God than you have said about yourself.- Henry Blackaby in Experiencing God

CHAPTER 27

A Troubled Season

Like virtually every American, I know exactly where I was when the twin towers came down. I was in the graphics department of my company, going over some orders and waiting for Pat Baker to call. We were scheduled to have lunch together.

Pat was Mary's boss. I'd talked with him on occasion at their office, and he'd lent me a chainsaw when ours broke. I knew he was successful in several different businesses. When I first met him, he was married. Now, having been separated for nearly two years, he was in the process of divorce. Mary cautioned me not to date him. She was afraid I might get hurt again.

That day Pat and I had decided to have lunch anyway. The television was on, with news of the catastrophe, all eyes and ears riveted to the story, most of us crying, when Pat called.

"If there's a TV in your office, you need to turn it on," he said,

"We're watching it now."

"Do you still want to meet for lunch?"

"I don't know."

I watched the screen for a moment, both of us silent, then he said, "Alicia's has a TV. Let's meet there."

We sat at Alicia's Restaurant watching the tragic news while we picked at our food, dumbfounded like everyone else in the world and desperately needing to share the experience with another soul.

In the months that followed, we dated a few times. I liked Pat very much, but my life was already crowded with too many commitments. I didn't have time for dating, and I told him so. We went to an Aggie football game and a charity dinner. I talked about the camp, the kids who came there, my children, my life. He talked about his family, his multitude of fascinating businesses, hobbies, and sports interests, especially basketball. One night after we finished dinner, Pat seemed particularly pensive.

"How important to you is your faith?" he asked, as he held my hand and twisted my silver cross pinkie ring round and round. The silence was pregnant.

"Extremely important," I whispered. "That's who I am. It's everything. It gives me purpose."

Pat didn't call after that, and I was okay about it. But I was lonely. On nearly every weekend the camp wasn't expecting a youth group, Scott and Jennifer drove to Dallas or Austin to visit his parents. Jeremy and Tina were now living in Austin. Nina had moved to an apartment in College Station, and we rarely spoke.

My back injury was still healing, and I had to be careful not to move too quickly. Most of the heavy work in taking care of the camp and campers, between March and May of that year, fell to Scott, Jennifer and Carol. Melissa came out faithfully every Friday to help us prepare for incoming guests. I took care of newsletters, mail-outs, and bookkeeping, and wondered what God was trying to teach me now.

"I could use a helpmate," I told Him once. "A partner who loves You as much as I do and shares my vision for the camp. Someone to rub my back when my back hurts. I'd do the same for him. Someone to care, someone to care for, someone to grow old with here at Cross Roads."

I didn't expect an answer, and I didn't get one. At least not right away.

The following February, I was invited to a dinner dance fundraiser benefiting the local hospital. I wanted to go, and not as a tagalong to a married couple. Although Pat and I had stopped dating months earlier, I decided to ask him to be my escort, only for that one evening. At the last minute, he was unable to attend, and I went alone.

The next day he invited me to dinner.

Dogwood Picnic

In every sales position I've held, my salary was among the highest on the sales staff. I preferred working for commission only, because the harder and smarter you work, the more money you make. After all, that's the whole point of having a job and I'm pretty good at sales.

But I'm not so good at asking for donations. Perhaps that's the reason I initially pursued Cross Roads as a business. I understand business. I also understand fundraising, intellectually, but I just don't have it in me to ask for money. It's hard enough to ask for help, and I only learned to do that because people were volunteering so readily.

Even after God convinced me that Cross Roads was not going to operate as a business, I balked at fundraising. If people wanted to donate money, that was great. I'd write articles for our newsletters soliciting donations, but I couldn't bring myself to ask for it directly. That's why we had auctions and other fundraising events. Now I was fighting off feelings of desperation that threatened to pull me under. We'd been trying to finish the camp for more than four years.

Bookings were holding steady. We had regular customers now, some coming for their third or fourth year. Word about Cross Roads was spreading and new folks came every season. The two cabins were warm and dry, but the only covered gathering place, the pavilion, still had no walls. The remnants of our building fund had gone to pour a slab, and the budget-draining events of last year had effectively shut down any other progress. We'd served plenty of meals to kids shivering on benches, shielding their plates from the rain slanting in under the roof. Still no kitchen, so we continued to cook at our homes and carry the food down to the camp. Yes, I understood now that Cross Roads wasn't about the facilities, and faith is about more than creature comforts, but having a warm dry place to eat sure would help.

Even some of our regulars decided that the risk of bad weather spoiling an important yearly retreat was not a risk they were willing to take. We needed to attract new people, but we also needed a fully sheltered facility to keep our old ones coming back, which meant getting serious about fundraising.

As we experienced the usual unpredictable weather that winter of 2001-2002, our Advisory Board brainstormed various fundraising ideas.

"We could expand the yearly picnic and turn it into a fundraiser," Cindy suggested.

"The Dogwood Picnic?" I asked, always wary of changes to an event that's working fine as is.

Spring in Central Texas is blessed with dogwood blossoms. Wildflowers turn the roadsides into a dazzling tapestry of color, red bud and wild plums trees add to the spectacle during those months, yet by far the showiest trees are the dogwoods. By the middle of March, Cross Roads bursts into bloom with white dogwood blossoms. The trees grow wild beneath the oaks, and for weeks the woods are filled with their gorgeous white flowers sparkling in the sunlight among the brown tree trunks and the dark green leaves of the undergrowth. Neighbors, friends, relatives and folks from all over the area come to Cross Roads to witness the magnificent yearly display. In prior years we had hosted a volunteer-and-donor appreciation event on the first weekend in April, which we called the Dogwood Picnic.

"People feel generous in the spring," Melissa agreed. "And a good season with lots of activity always inspires folks to want to be part of what's happening out here. Hopefully, they'll contribute to our new building plans."

"Not exactly new," I had to point out. "Cross Roads has needed an enclosed dining hall since day one."

"Then maybe this is the year God will make it happen."

"I can create a visual," Jean Bailey, a member of my Accountability Group, suggested. "I can show exactly what we need and encourage people to donate funds for specific building materials." Accustomed to using her Ph. D. to promote the TurboLab at Texas A&M, she'd have to scale down her ideas considerably to match our budget. I was sure she could do it. Jean had been a welcome advisor on our board for three years.

"I think I can get a great band this year," I said. My brother-in-law, Dan Dickson, was in a terrific praise-and-worship band called "Godsong."

A plan began to take shape. Carol immediately drew up a menu. When I told Pat about the fundraiser, he solicited sausages from Slovacek's in Snook. We compiled lists and sent out more invitations than ever before. With careful preparation and God's blessing, this would be our biggest, most successful fundraiser ever.

Diehards

As the weekend approached, we kept a wary eye on the weather. It occurred to me at one point that the success of this event would guarantee we'd never suffer the whim of Texas weather in the future. Thus far, we seemed fated to have every big event rained out. Unfortunately, the forecast for the weekend was grim. Heavy weather off to the west was moving in our direction.

Saturday dawned bright and sunny, so our spirits were high that morning. Melissa came to help Scott, Jennifer, and me mow, clean, and set up the tables and chairs.

Dan Dickson and his fellow band members arrived, pulling a trailer full of musical instruments and equipment. When I showed them where they'd be playing, their eyebrows shot up. Exchanging furtive looks, the band set up at the edge of the open-air pavilion, while Dan pulled me quietly aside.

"You think the weather will hold?" he asked.

"We're praying for it." I flashed my most assuring smile.

"Okay." He shrugged, unconvinced, before rushing off to reassure the other band members.

Jean showed up next proudly displaying a giant poster that identified every item needed to enclose the pavilion. Listed individually, each door, window, doorknob, box of nails, HardiPlank exterior board, roll of insulation, piece of sheetrock, or stack of two-by-fours boasted a ribbon with a price tag attached. She had designed the list to include at least one item to fit everyone's price range. A good breeze was blowing now, ushering a scent of rain in the air, so she positioned her display in a protected area at the back of the pavilion by the only wall.

Pat arrived with the donated sausages and a wide banner promoting Slovacek's Sausage Company, which he displayed prominently as promised. Carol lit the charcoal and everyone helped her set out the food and tableware. We loaded the buffet table with trays of brownies, watermelon, chips, and bowls of Carol's now famous salsa. No Cross Roads event was complete without Carol's salsa.

Shortly before noon we gathered around and prayed for a successful day. Then the band cranked up the music, playing favorite praise-and-worship oldies as well as some of their original compositions. Folks straggled in. Relatives, including my mom and dad, drove up from Houston. Cindy's family came from LaGrange, bringing her brother who was visiting from Pennsylvania.

The Dogwoods began to sway as the wind whistled through their limbs sending flurries of white petals across the yard. Big drops of rain pelted the dry ground around the pavilion, exploding puffs of dirt.

Soon, the drops turned to sheets. Rivulets of water snaked across the concrete slab. Pat grabbed a long janitor's broom and tried shoving the water away from the band's electrical equipment, only to see it follow his broom right back in. The band members bravely played on, with one eye on the encroaching water and the other on their music. As the wind whipped rain under the pavilion's roof, folks dashed for their cars.

In the end, the only people, besides relatives, who came and stayed at that picnic were the diehards, the ones who knew us, believed in Cross Roads, and had been there at every other event. Our biggest fundraiser ever ended as a dismal failure.

"When we were talking about New York last night and the fire was burning it made me think of how you have to value life."

- Logan, after 9/11

Like the winds of the sea are the ways of fate
As we voyage along through life,
'Tis the set of a soul
That decides its goal
And not the calm or the strife.

- Ella Wheeler

CHAPTER 28

Scraping Up the Pieces

While the rest of us huddled in gloom, replaying the event in our conversations, generously riddled with "if onlys," Pat turned his remarkable business mind toward more fruitful processes. Early that summer, he had commented on the tractor-trailer parked in the yard overflowing with building materials, equipment, and salvaged supplies slowly going to ruin.

"What are you planning to do with all that?" he asked.

"I don't know," I admitted. "Jennifer says I should get rid of it. The idea was to get additional building materials donated and to use these items when we build a kitchen and enclose the pavilion."

"Meanwhile, our front 'yard' resembles the junkyard in the Sandford and Son television series, only on steroids."

"It's been sitting there a while."

"Let it go, Hilda. Auction everything off for whatever you can get and put the money in the bank."

He was right, of course. Many of the items we'd never use anyway, and the others might be too far gone by the time we were ready to build. So we put together another work detail to tally up the entire collection and set a starting bid for each piece. Ellen Knight, another dear friend from my Accountability Group acted as cashier while the auctioneer skillfully auctioned off the items, raising $6,500 for the building fund. It wasn't exactly a windfall, but it sweetened our account nicely, as well as our dispositions.

Change Is In the Wind

After the failure of our fundraising picnic, I brooded for hours, reviewing the past two years, which I felt had spun us backwards in many ways. I saw a long chain of calamities and setbacks, and the common thread, from my point of view, was my lack of concentrated effort. How could I adequately affect what was happening with Cross Roads when I spent most of my week working at a totally unrelated job? My abilities in sales and marketing were exhausted by my current job.

If I focused that skill on promoting Cross Roads, by calling on church staff, speaking at various churches, and making an all-out effort to put the word out, I knew I could make a difference. We could attract more youth groups from possibly bigger, more affluent churches. We were limited by our facility, true, but we could accommodate more youths, more frequently, than we were at present.

The only way to make that happen, I decided, was to stop baby-stepping and take a giant leap. If I quit my day job, I could dedicate my full-time effort to the vision God has placed on my heart.

When I told Jennifer and Scott what I intended to do, they didn't disagree, but they were noticeably quiet about it.

"The camp is bringing in enough revenue now to pay me a modest salary," I explained. "A far cry from the multiple salaries we envisioned four years ago, but enough for food and essentials. With that support, I can spend time marketing Cross Roads and still have time to take care of the day-to-day chores."

"If that's what you think you need to do, go ahead," Scott said.

"We haven't put out newsletters consistently in a while," I added. "We haven't nearly explored all the churches within driving distance. With this extra time, I can do both."

"If it's what you want to do," Jennifer said ambiguously, "then you'll make it work. If anybody can do it, Mom, you can."

They didn't actually encourage me, but they didn't try to talk me out of it. I knew they felt as strongly as I did that we were running in circles going the way we were now.

Before May was over, I had turned in my resignation at the printing company. I was ready and eager to devote the summer touting Cross Roads to anyone who would listen.

Shortly thereafter, Jennifer and Scott came to me with the saddest faces I'd ever seen. Scott nervously hung back while Jennifer stepped forward.

"This isn't easy for us to tell you," she said. "We believe in what God is trying to accomplish here, and we want Cross Roads to succeed, but ..."

She paused as if waiting for me to speak. I froze, waiting for the other shoe to drop.

"We can't stay here any longer," she continued after a moment. "We have the kids, and they need a real home to grow up in. We need to move on. We'll still come here and help whenever we can."

I understood what they were telling me, but my brain refused to accept it. Myriad emotions rushed through me flooding my senses and rendering me incapable of voicing my feelings. Yes, I understood they needed a change in the way things were going as much as I did, but this blow took me to my knees.

Raging Inside

As soon as I was away from them, out of hearing range, all the questions I'd wanted to ask exploded angrily into dead lonely space.

"Why now?" We'd come so far, worked so hard. God had brought us so close. Despite the hard labor and the countless difficulties we'd dealt with, our time together had been purposeful and joyful. We were a team.

"How can you turn your back on God's calling in your lives? God tapped each of us on the shoulder, not just me. Cross Roads would never have worked if he'd called only me." We had experienced so many of His blessings together, had recounted them frequently, acknowledging each door God opened for us, each step that appeared frightening and impossible until He miraculously lighted the way. Could they really walk away from all that?

"How do you expect me to replace you? I'm not a teacher like Jennifer, and I don't have Scott's physical strength or know-how!" Jennifer was the author of all our programs, and truly one of the most gifted teachers I've ever witnessed. I had a lot of gifts, but teaching kids was not among them. Scott was my anchor, my go-to-guy for everything that needed fixing, with a remarkable talent for figuring out how to get things done. I couldn't pick up that slack.

We'd laughed and shed tears together. They helped hold me together, literally, when I felt my life spinning out of control. Together, we barely had enough energy to accomplish what needed to be done each week. Neither of them was replaceable, and even if I could find the right people, there was no money to pay for those skills, and nobody would be as crazy as we were to do it all for free. How could I possibly complete what we started without them?

Jennifer and Scott were not the only targets for my rantings. I also raged at God.

"Why would You bring us this far only to let this happen? You know I can't do this alone! I've poured my heart, soul, health, every ounce of energy, and every penny into pursuing Your mission. What do You expect from me now?"

I'd weathered enough counseling to know that the root cause for that much anger is fear. I was afraid that my family's criticism would finally be proven true, that from the start Cross Roads was a failure waiting to happen. Not only had my family called me crazy, they'd thought I was criminal for dragging Nina through this, taking her out of school, expecting her to sleep on the back porch with plywood for walls and a space heater to keep her warm. Nina thought it was fun, at first.

Scott's parents had been equally critical. Their son, whom they were so proud of for landing an excellent job right out of college at a prestigious magazine, was turning his back on his executive path to corporate success. He was shucking his three-piece suits in favor of ratty jeans and driving a tractor. Living with his mother-in-law, working for nothing, what was he thinking? I suspected that they'd pressured him often to return to 'sanity'.

So now everybody had a chance to say, "I told you so." Nina had gotten pregnant, moved away, and was barely speaking to me. And although I hadn't realized it, Jennifer and Scott were on the verge of divorce. Over these six years, I'd failed to fully appreciate the stress they suffered trying to heal and hold onto their marriage under the difficult conditions we lived in at Cross Roads.

Was I on the wrong path? Obviously, I'd failed my children, and without their continued contributions to this quest, Cross Roads would certainly go under. I'd be forced out.

In the end, had I failed God, too?

*Two are better than one, because they have a good
reward for their toil. For if they fall, one will lift up his
fellow. But woe to him who is alone when he falls and
has not another to lift him up! - Ecclesiastes 4:9-10*

CHAPTER 29

Bottomed Out

My Accountability Group got an earful at our next meeting. As
usual, they helped me refocus.

"I can't do it alone," I told them.

"Have you asked for help?"

Asking for help never came easy for me. "Finding a program
leader is not the same as asking someone to help fix the roof.
There's no money to pay for that kind of talent."

"Jennifer created a number of programs over the years. Did
she write them down?"

Of course she had. "I suppose we can follow her directions,
do the programs the way she wrote them."

I still didn't know who "we" might be.

"What if this time it's impossible?" I knew I was wallowing in
misery and self-pity, but that's where I was at the moment, and
these were my friends. "There's so little money and so much to
do. Am I being obstinate refusing to admit I failed?"

"You haven't failed until you quit."

Hearing them say it gave me the boost I needed. The truth was, as little as I had to show for six years of hardships and toil, these had been the happiest, most exhilarating years of my entire life.

I still believed Cross Roads was what I was supposed to be doing. God doesn't change His mind in midstream about something He wants done, and it was still an exciting adventure for me. As long as I had food to eat, a roof over my head, I could keep moving forward.

What I could not do was walk away. When I thought about closing that door on my life and walking away from it, my heart sank, empty and dead.

I recalled His voice, as I'd heard it that day sitting on a swing under the spreading branches of a Texas oak. "You can do this. I will be with you." He did not say, "Jennifer and Scott will be with you."

I don't believe anyone who has *not* heard His voice or felt His touch can quite understand. It's different from any earthly experience. It's mystical. It's powerful. It's supernatural. It changes you from inside out, and there's no turning back.

I might be forced out. I might run off track, lose everything. I might die. I might eventually fail, but it wasn't going to happen because I gave up on God.

No Expectations

Having made up my mind to keep going, I now needed a new plan. Without Jennifer and Scott, it was more important than ever for me to get busy bringing in money. Fortunately, this was summertime, our off-season. Since I no longer had a paying job to report to every morning, what I did have was time.

Right away, I resumed the newsletter and mail-outs, not as fancy as when Scott designed them, but they'd have to do. I called on churches anywhere within driving distance, using my sales skills to schedule fall and winter retreats.

Pat phoned fairly frequently to ask me out, but I didn't have much time for him.

"There's a stack of bookkeeping to do, and that's not my strong suit, so it takes me awhile." Having dinner out actually sounded like fun, but it meant making myself presentable, which wasn't a high priority when you lived deep in the woods and didn't expect to see anyone. Usually, I was too tired to eat out anyway.

Admittedly, I missed the daily adult companionship I'd had with Scott and Jennifer. And I really liked Pat.

I recalled the first time I'd dropped by to see Mary, entering the offices through the back door, and Pat was standing there, six-foot-three-inches tall, about 250 pounds, and altogether daunting.

"I'm looking for Mary Stevens," I stammered, thinking, *man, he's big*.

"Right over here." He led me to the second office on the right.

A moment later, Mary introduced us, and I learned that Pat was her boss. She was his assistant. His office was the first one on the right, which I passed every time I visited her after that.

He had an impressive antique roll-top desk, his walls were covered with geological and seismic data charts, and he was always wheeling and dealing on the phone. And when he was on the phone, he was usually pacing. He'd look up, say "Hi," and go back to work. The energy generating from that office was palpable.

Pat was married back then, so to me he was just Mary's boss, but he seemed to be an interesting person, a smart businessman, and most importantly, highly competent. Friendly, easy going, he never minded that I'd come by to visit. And he occasionally popped over to Mary's office to say hello.

That was in the early days of Cross Roads, late 1996. By the time Pat asked me out to lunch in September of 2001, he was in the process of divorce and I was recovering from a broken back. After the charity dance I invited him to in February, we started dating again and continued throughout that spring. One day, out of the blue, he said, "When are you going to ask me to go to church with you?"

Panicked by the thought of what people would think if I showed up in church with another man, and remembering our former conversation on this subject, when he'd asked me about the importance of faith in my life, I froze. Once again, I had been challenged to put my money where my mouth was. He enjoyed church, and everybody liked him. Soon afterward, he joined the church and had rapidly become involved.

Now, in the summer of 2002, I devoted most days to the camp, working alone except for the Fridays when Melissa volunteered. Pat no longer seemed so daunting, and in fact, we were dating seriously. But feeling the weight of the entire mission on my shoulders, I couldn't afford to be distracted.

On the other hand, having a successful businessman to bounce ideas around with counted more as a help than a distraction. Besides, I liked his eyes. It had been many years since I could look forward to social functions knowing a handsome man would accompany me. As a single adult, I was rarely invited to social occasions in our community, and when I was, I'd invariably gone as Scott and Jennifer's third wheel. All I was looking for now was someone to have dinner with occasionally, visit with, maybe take in a movie. I was attracted to Pat, but not blown away.

What I did not want was a man involved in my life at Cross Roads. I didn't need or want a man taking care of me or trying to take over.

Changing Gears

If you get into a game with an alpha male, you have to expect him to try and grab the ball and run with it. Pat was keenly interested in the camp, as both a new Christian and as my friend.

"The camp needs a conference room and a chapel," he informed me. "And more cabins."

"We need a bunch of stuff," I agreed warily. He was right, yet I didn't want him thinking he had to solve my problems. "We don't even have a dining room. We have an open-air pavilion on a concrete slab. But we'll get there eventually, one baby step at a time."

Pat went to work, and he doesn't work in baby steps. He travels in circles with very successful friends, so when he shared his newfound passion with them donations poured in. One of his business partners was a homebuilder and had access to contractors. Pat negotiated for the contractors to donate their labor if we bought the materials. He went from zero to ninety overnight, all the while being incredibly patient with me, because I was resistant about letting him in. I kept having to remind myself that this was God's camp, not mine, and He could use anybody He wanted to build it.

At our next board meeting, I mentioned that my biggest obstacle was providing the programming.

"Jennifer left excellent written materials," I said, "but that's only part of what she did so well. She would have those kids enthralled. I could try, but –"

"What would happen if you didn't offer programming?" someone asked.

"Our whole strategy has been based on our programming." I instantly felt my resistance rising. "We market to small churches that don't have a youth director and that need the programs we offer."

"But what if you started marketing to larger churches, those that do have a youth director? Is that impossible?"

"The two cabins will only sleep about forty," I argued.

"There must be a middle ground, churches that are not too big or too small."

Change, like asking for help, doesn't come easy for me, but I had to admit they had a point. In the early days, when we had no cabins, the groups had to be small and our programming was the main attraction. With Jennifer and Scott gone, was God pointing me in a new direction? Maybe He wanted me to set aside the notion of providing programs.

I started calling on larger churches and discovered this new strategy came with a bonus: larger, more affluent churches were as easy to attract as smaller ones, and they could afford larger fees.

Then Pat dropped a bomb in my lap: he proposed.

> "It brought me God and many good feelings. I felt safe and comfortable. I prayed for my parents and that both will find God."
>
> - Dalton, talking about Cross Roads

I spent sixty-plus years thinking I had to have all the answers to everything. Whatever needed handling, I relied on myself to be able to handle it. I worked with some strong associates, and we did whatever we needed to do. There were things missing in my life, but I didn't know how to admit it, or how to change it. I was just going down the road.

When I met Hilda, I thought there was a possibility she was crazy, or at least misguided. I saw how she butted her head against the wall over and over. Through Mary, I knew what was going on at times, when this or that wasn't going well. For a long while, I heard the stories and thought Hilda was putting an awful lot of energy into a pipe dream. I felt there were more rewarding things she could be doing with that energy, things she could touch, see, or spend.

Then one day Hilda had a tree down and needed a chainsaw. I owned a chainsaw. When she borrowed it, she was bubbly and warm. Her personality did not seem to be that of a crazy person, not totally crazy, anyway. And I was attracted.

It was quite some time before we began seriously dating. After we'd been dating for a while I could see how important her faith was, how much she relied on her relationship with Christ for guidance.

Then one day, I said, "Are you going to ask me to church?"

I really wanted to go, because that was a big part of her life, and at that point I was interested in whatever was in her life. I wanted to be a part of it. She hesitated, but eventually said, "Yes. Come with me to church next Sunday."

Church quickly became a habit. It was something we shared and looked forward to. I enjoyed the sermons and the choral music. I joined some classes.

I experienced a tremendous amount of growth. At first, I wasn't much of a fellowship guy. I joke about it now that I was living the doctrine of "Fake it 'til you make it." Eventually I became committed to evangelism but still didn't really care, or maybe I just didn't think about other people enough. I've always had great friendships, fraternity brothers, and I stayed in touch, but that wasn't the same. I could see that Hilda really cared about what she was doing because she cared about the people who would ultimately benefit.

Spiritually, Cross Roads is an important part of the whole of my Christian experience. The church, Emmaus, and everything we do come together in that regard. But at Cross Roads, we express better than anywhere else the quality of servant-hood. If a person truly believes, as I do, in Christian love, then servant-hood is part of it. During a sermon or talk I gave once, I used the line that "Servant-hood is love in action." At Cross Roads we get a chance to express that love twenty-five to thirty weekends a year.

The groups themselves are a part of the faith experience. To see their reverence, their worship, is inspiring. I remember in particular a group that prayed with us at the spot where we're going to make a Prayer Garden in memory of Hilda's mother. That was truly a once-in-a-lifetime experience.

Some of my friends and family have never come to terms with where I am now spiritually. They probably think I'm nuts, the same as I thought about her. On the other hand, they see that I'm serious. It has become who I am. They see that I don't use bad language anymore around the office. It's my part of a commitment to living a Christian life. When I say I have to be at Cross Roads, or at Emmaus, they see that I'm serious about my spirituality, and they respect that. I believe they respect me more.

Emotionally, Cross Roads brings both highs and lows. Obviously, the highs come with the groups, with the privilege of sharing their discoveries, and there are many more highs than lows.

But one significant low I recall was the Dogwood Picnic. We were all set for a big deal, a significant event, to raise a lot of money to enclose the dining hall. Our expectations were high.

It rained all day. Hardly anybody came, and those that did come probably ate more than they donated, which was all right, except that I knew it was disappointing for Hilda. At one point during the day, I saw Hilda sitting alone on her swing, and I felt so bad for her.

That was the first time I ever prayed hard. I prayed for her not to feel so badly about the way it was going and for God's help to make it happen. She was dedicated and upbeat about it, but I could feel her disappointment. I realized that I cared more about what happened to Hilda and how she felt than I did about me. That was probably a first.

Fundraising was something I understood well. Since God needed this work done, needed these facilities, then I knew I needed to get involved in the fundraising process.

Every weekend at Cross Roads we were blessing people, not only the campers, but also the volunteers, all the people who work there, and they knew it. They felt it. They expressed it. It's joyful work joyfully received. And that's pretty uncommon. That's not ordinary, at all. Being part of that, being part of putting it together was important. I was needed here.

In the first letter I wrote to raise funds for the cabins and enclosing the dining hall, I talked about seeing the joy on the faces of the campers. I guess it worked, because we raised about $25,000. It was easy, because I'd seen it, I'd been a part of it, and it was obviously what God wanted.

Cross Roads is a constant blessing. It keeps me active and is helping me get into better physical shape. I mow, make fires, chop firewood, cut brush.

I remember Hilda asking, right in the middle of building the chapel, if I'd thought I'd be building a chapel at age sixty-five. I said "no," because obviously I hadn't.

But this was a big part of my spiritual awakening, and it's an important part of my life, our life. It's hard to separate Hilda and Cross Roads. It's such a big part of who she is. At the same time, being married to her and being part of Cross Roads is not the same thing. Cross Roads has its own rewards. Being married to Hilda has others.

This last year, it seemed like every time we had a camp I needed to be somewhere else. But I still wanted to go down and work. So I'd go sometimes at seven-thirty a.m. only to leave an hour later. I want to be a part of it, and I miss it when I'm not.

I've changed a lot. It says in the liturgy, "the mystery of faith," and that's exactly what it means. The day I finally understood that fact was a turning point in my Christianity. I know now that a person doesn't need to have all the answers. You just need faith. And even when you can't touch, see, or spend the results of your work, when you care about people and you experience with them the reverence and joy of worship, you definitely feel it. You feel that joy not only in the big moments but also in the smallest moments, and in every inch of your physical being.

So they are no longer two, but one. - Matthew 19:6

CHAPTER 30

Yes, But...

Although I knew it was coming, after all, a relationship can't remain static it's either growing or dying - Pat's proposal caught me by surprise. I had to go sit on the couch for a moment, an asthma attack stealing my breath.

Pat says he has no memory of that, and men remember events differently than women do, but we both recall that I had reservations. I loved Pat, and I knew we needed to do this, yet I was closed off to the idea of letting another man so completely into my new world. I couldn't believe I was brave enough to even consider going there again.

For the first time in my life I had close friendships with women I loved and depended upon, women who magically appeared at my side during any important occasion. They worked beside me at the camp. They sat by my bed at the hospital. They brought meals to my home when I was recovering from a broken back. They counseled me, cried with me, celebrated with me. I didn't want that part of my life to change.

And this mission I'd undertaken, it was God's work, yes, but it was also *mine*. I was the one He had called to steer this ship, and during these years of good times and bad, I was hardheaded enough to keep my hand always at the wheel. Change had come the hard way.

Previously, in my childhood as well as my marriages, men took control of my life. That never worked for me. Believing I was in control had proved equally disastrous. The only thing that did work for me was giving God control of my life.

Pat was stronger by far than any man I'd ever known. By marrying him, I was agreeing to share my world, to share the camp and the vision God had given me for it. Could I do that? If he'd come into my life five years earlier, the answer would have been a resounding "no." But I believed I had grown to a point where I was strong enough to tell him when to back off. I also believed that he was mature enough to hear it.

Pat was competent, which I valued in a man, goodhearted, and extremely fair. One thing that attracted me when we first started dating was the fair and generous manner in which he'd handled his divorce. He didn't talk about it much, but Bryan/College Station is a small community, and you hear things. He was extremely caring and generous in that situation, determined to not just meet the letter of the law, but to go beyond that, to ensure that his family was well provided for.

I'd never experienced any generosity like that in my life. For him, that was just the natural way to be, the right way to handle a complicated situation, but for me it marked him as a man I could trust.

And hadn't I prayed for such a relationship? The years with Scott and Jennifer were wonderful, but at times I envied them. They had each other. Secretly, in the past few years, I had asked God to send me helpmate, a man I could love and trust enough to share this new life that God had given me.

God must have known that I had to evolve to the point where I was ready, strong enough, willing and able, to accept a man like Pat into my life. Since I'm notoriously obstinate, it took a lot for me to get there. I believe now that everything I went through before I met Pat was part of God's very gradual loosening of my grip on the steering wheel, one finger at a time. Like the woman in Shakespeare's play, "The Taming of the Shrew," I was humbled until I was able to appreciate not having to be in total control, willing to *share* control.

So Pat and I came together at the right time and right place. He was quite probably the only man in the world who fit my criteria, a man I could love and meet eye-to-eye on level ground. I would rather walk over hot coals than mess that up.

Would uttering those two dangerous little words change the balance we had created between us?

Saying those two dangerous little words

Do You Take this Man …?

Spring is absolutely the most beautiful time at Cross Roads. With the dogwoods in full bloom, the Outdoor Sanctuary is a gorgeous spot for a wedding. My friends decorated the newly enclosed dining hall with dogwood boughs for the reception. Carol provided food, Jennifer baked and decorated the cake. Mary stood next to the pastor, singing *a cappella,* a solo Pat had requested, "Surely the Presence Of the Lord Is In this Place."

But even as I stood waiting to walk down the aisle between the cedar benches, my brain whirled with doubt. What was I doing here … in this situation … again? Why should I believe marriage would work for me this time, when it never had before? Did I really know this man? I hadn't known he played bass guitar until our pastor told me Pat had signed up to play in the praise band at church.

You know his heart came the answer inside my head.

Did I? I knew he'd led a full and colorful life before we met. I knew he made his first fortune working for one of the earliest computer companies in the world, selling used computers as big as a room. When US technology advanced, Pat would sell the old computers to countries just getting to that point. I knew he'd been on the Merv Griffin show modeling some old NASA spacesuits he was trying to sell to the Russians. I knew he was one of the original founders and part owner of an Italian restaurant in Vail, Colorado. I knew he was in the oil and gas business. I knew he'd won trophies racing sailboats, bass fishing, and breeding and showing sheep dogs. I knew he had received a plaque from *ABC's Wide World of Sports* for bowling a perfect 300 game. I knew he flew his own plane, had been into harness racing, and had owned a horse that won a million-dollar purse. Pat was an interesting and successful man, but none of what had come before was important to me. What was important was knowing that Pat never did anything halfway. He does his homework, gives a hundred percent, and achieves excellence. I knew he would put that same hundred-percent effort into this marriage.

You couldn't have picked a stronger personality to marry, the voice cautioned.

Yes, but I'm strong now, too, so we'll do well together. For one thing, nothing will ever intimidate Pat or threaten his masculinity. In the praise band, when the music warms everyone's hearts, Pat's the one up there with tears in his eyes. In the Bible study I led, called "Chocolate for Lent," by Hilary Brand, Pat was one of only three men who attended. The rest were women. He's strong enough to be tender when it counts. Pat is a dominant individual who does not have to dominate.

It will never be perfect.

Perfect would be too scary to imagine. We all have to be constantly improving ourselves. That's one thing I adore about Pat. He's always growing and learning and doing. I respect that. And he's honest about it. So few people can be honest about who they are and what they need to accomplish. Yes, there will be trials, and we'll have our disagreements. He'll want to do something one way, and I'll have a different idea. If it has to do with the camp, I'll say, "You've got fifteen other businesses, stay out of mine." I couldn't have said that years ago, and be heard. Pat listens. I can be myself with Pat. When we decided to marry, we agreed that the most important factor for both of us was having somebody we could work with. For me, that's as perfect as it gets.

Holding hands now, Pat and I walked down the wooded prayer trail, between the cedar benches in the outdoor sanctuary, where our family and friends sat, and I remembered an important conversation. Pat's from Missouri, and I knew he had planned to return there when he retired. "I'm not leaving Texas," I told him. "So there's no future for this relationship." My hopes for us back then were not long term. "In fact, I don't plan to live anywhere but Cross Roads for the rest of my life." Pat didn't argue with me, but I wasn't sure we'd actually resolved that issue.

As Mary's song ended, we faced the pastor, and then each other, as the minister said the magic words that would change my world forever. I looked into Pat's face, and those remarkable eyes that had so attracted me, and I recalled another of our conversations.

I had asked him what made him decide he wanted to marry me. Pat said he'd reached a point in his life where he had all the money he needed or could ever want, had engaged in every hobby he could imagine pursuing, had acquired everything he needed, yet was still looking. He was empty. Something was missing in his life.

The he met me, and I had nothing, had lost everything, was all alone, but he'd never met anyone happier. He wanted what I had. And what I had was Christ.

"I do," I said, and I meant it with my heart, soul, every fiber of my being,

Take courage! It is I. Don't be afraid. - Mark 6:51

CHAPTER 31

Listen and You Will Hear ...

The fall before our wedding, Pat and I facilitated two youth retreats together. We did our best, we followed Jennifer's outlines faithfully, but they were only outlines. Without her spontaneity the effort was doomed.

After the second group drove away, Pat said, "We can't do programs. That part of Cross Roads is over. At least for now."

"The programs are a huge part of our mission," I argued.

I proceeded to explain in detail, although he'd heard it all before, how we had come to Cross Roads thinking it was about the buildings and learned that it was about the people and the programs that brought kids closer to understanding Christ's love.

"We can't do programs," he repeated. "That's not our talent."

"Then we might as well close it down."

No, I didn't really mean it and I wasn't being realistic. Besides, the Board had hashed this out months ago, coming to the same conclusion, and I had, in fact, booked several youth groups from churches large enough to have a program director. They came, they paid bigger fees, and they were totally self-sufficient.

But I still wanted to offer the camp, complete with programming, to those smaller groups who needed it. I enjoyed the interaction. Building a bonfire is not the same when you build it and then leave before the good part starts. And running a retreat is not as much fun when you're in the kitchen the entire time washing dishes.

"First, it was about the facility," I grumbled to Pat. "Then we realized it was about the people and the programs. With the programs gone, it's about the facility again."

"If you ask me, I'd say God's pretty happy with Cross Roads. As long as you keep the electricity on, the Holy Spirit will do the rest."

I laughed. "You mean, it's not all about me?"

Pat and I were learning how to engage in such discussions without either of us getting all in a tizzy about it. I was okay with him saying, as he did quite often, "You can't do that. It won't work," as long as he listened when I said, "Well, it worked in the past."

The important thing was knowing his heart was in the right place. He had jumped into the Cross Roads mission with both feet. His first fundraising letter brought in enough to enclose the pavilion and add the kitchen.

Pat's Angels

Fundraising became Pat's primary mission, self-imposed and much appreciated. Money trickled in faster than it ever had before, $1,000, $2,000, or $5,000 at a whack. But Pat's plan was to keep building until we had a facility that would accommodate the size groups that would make Cross Roads financially viable.

The summer after our wedding, he connected me with his friend, George Smith, who lived in Charlotte, North Carolina. George had known Pat forever and practically considered him a son. Now he wanted to meet the woman Pat had married and find out more about this camp called Cross Roads.

So Pat and I flew out to meet George and his wife, Emily, a true Southern Belle. Both exuded southern hospitality. George was ninety-odd years old but quick, sharp, with a keen interest in all sorts of business ventures. He had owned the first franchise distributorship for Titleist Golf Balls. He was also into oil and gas, and was one of Pat's investors.

He'd taken us to his club for dinner, and we were headed back to our hotel. Pat and I rode in the back seat, with George driving.

"Tomorrow morning," George drawled in his gentlemanly southern accent, "I want you all to come by the office."

"Oh, now, George," Emily said, before Pat or I could answer, "Hilda doesn't have any interest in listening to you two men talk business. You just take Pat. Hilda and I are going shopping. Hilda, you'd rather go shopping with me, wouldn't you?"

I sincerely had wanted to meet Pat's dear friends, but my other reason for being there was that George was considering a major donation to the camp. Emily, bless her heart, had just pulled the rug out from under me. I was caught between the proverbial rock and a hard place.

"Ms. Emily," I said, "whatever you and George decide is fine with me."

The next morning, George called.

"Hilda, Ms. Emily is not feeling well right now, so why don't you come with Pat up to the office?"

George's office was straight out of the 1950s, obviously an executive workplace with the skinny-legged desk, credenza, and other furnishings popular in that era. We talked about how I had come to Cross Roads, what we hoped to accomplish, and I shared stories of the many "God things" that had happened along the way.

After a while, George opened a drawer, pulled out a manila folder, and extracted a stack of municipal bonds and stock certificates. He licked a finger and started counting them off the top.

"How much do you need, Hilda? Ten thousand? Twenty? Thirty?"

I asked Pat later if my mouth was hanging open. I know I was holding my breath, expecting a hand to reach out and shake me awake.

I walked out of George's office that day with $50,000 in negotiable bonds, and later met Ms. Emily at a dress shop, where she picked out a ruffled pink chiffon dress, not at all my style, for me to wear to Nina's wedding. Pat loved it, though, so I wore it proudly.

George's incredibly generous donation enabled us to build a cabin that same summer.

The Labyrinth

Carol attracted another angel to Cross Roads that summer, and another $50,000 anonymous donation. All her life, this angel had wanted a Cadillac and never got one, yet she was generously donating an amount equal to that dream so that Cross Roads could accommodate more campers.

We named the new structure the Cadillac Cabin and installed a plaque inscribed with Matthew 6:19 which reads, "Do not store up for yourselves treasures on earth, where moth and rust destroy, and where thieves break in and steal."

With enough money now to buy building materials, and Pat's contractors donating their services at cost, we didn't have to be there hammering and sawing, for a change. Watching what a team of competent construction workers can do in a day was exhilarating.

Without my hands-on help, the two new cabins went up and the dining hall interior was finished. Meanwhile, instead of lazing around, I spent my summer calling on churches that in the past had exceeded our capacity. When the fall arrived, we were decked out and ready for our busiest season ever.

One crisp morning, I was talking to Melissa and a subject came up that I had toyed with for quite some time.

"A Labyrinth?" Melissa said. "I had no idea you were interested in Labyrinths."

"God put it on my heart to build one, but I've never found anyone who knows how. Even Pat just scratched his head when he saw the math involved, and not much confuses him."

My first introduction to the subject had occurred on another crisp morning, a Saturday a year or so earlier. The new camp kitchen was bustling with a few early risers, mostly adults, already nursing hot cups of coffee. Carol was barking orders.

"Have you put the juices out?"

"Yes, we did." The volunteer kitchen helpers, including me, scurried to finish setting up the buffet.

"How about the hot sauce?"

"Yes."

"Did you remember to cover the muffins?"

The camp bell rang loudly, summoning fifty or so teens and their counselors to circle up for a prayer. Their *Amen* signaled a mad scramble to fall in line for a hot breakfast. As they passed the serving window one by one, our volunteers greeted the kids with cheerful faces and plates heaping with Carol's breakfast tacos.

One young lady paused just long enough to ask, "Do you have a labyrinth?"

"A what?" I replied.

Shrugging, she moved on. I was too busy to give it a second thought.

A few months later, another group of teens called me over to their table.

"Do you have a labyrinth?" one of them asked.

"What, exactly, *is* a labyrinth?"

They explained that it looked like a maze, but was different.

"There's only one route in and back out again. No blind alleys, no dead ends, no tricks like you'd find in a maze."

They further explained that labyrinths had been used over the centuries as a tool for prayer, meditation, and for personal and spiritual growth.

"Cross Roads is a *perfect* place for one," a boy commented.

"It'd be really cool if you built it out in the woods somewhere," said another boy.

The third time came a few weeks later, when in wide-eyed amazement I read about a labyrinth in my church newsletter. The district's Prayer Labyrinth was being set up in our church fellowship hall the following week.

"Okay, God, I got it. You want a labyrinth at Cross Roads."

The following week, I was one of the first people to show up. The church parlor, which connects to the Fellowship Hall, had become the reception area. One of our church members, who was knowledgeable about labyrinths, was there to answer questions.

After signing the guest book, I slowly read the information provided.

- There is one path in, and you follow the same path out. Move at your own pace.

- If someone wants to pass you, briefly step aside.

- Walk slowly and reflectively or energetically, there is no "right way" to walk the path.

- Be intentional while walking the labyrinth. Think of a question or issue that concerns you. Pray for a person or a situation. Pray about a spiritual question, vocational issues, healing for a relationship, or health. Pray with gratitude, or about confusion or fear you may be experiencing. Pray for guidance.

- Spend as long as you want in the center.

- This is a canvas labyrinth, so please remove your shoes.

A basketful of clean white socks sat waiting for those who needed them.

What the instructions didn't say, but what I surmised, was this: Be still, listen, and you may hear His voice, feel His touch. It sounded pretty heavy, as if I were getting ready to meet God in person. I couldn't help feeling apprehensive.

When I opened the door to the Fellowship Hall, the soft haunting rhythm of chanting monks enveloped me, and the candlelit Prayer Labyrinth sprawled out before me. I stood for a moment admiring the beauty and serenity that lay waiting.

Walking slowly to the entrance, I paused and asked God to send His Holy Spirit to meet me. Then I stepped in.

As I prayed and walked, the winding path took me along the edge, then inward, toward the center, then back to the edge. Just when I thought I'd make it to center, the path spun me off in another direction, over and over again, in and out and all around. The direction I followed was completely unpredictable. I quit anticipating and tried to simply go with the Labyrinth's flow.

Unexpectedly, I found myself at the center. Powerful warmth surged through me. My knees weakened and I knelt down abruptly. Kneeling there in the heart of that circuitous path, I felt serene yet energized. In a moment of astounding clarity, I realized that the path replicated the stops and starts of my life, and that the path to God is not straight but full of twists and turns. The only sure thing was that God is at the center of the universe waiting for us. All we have to do is stay on the path and keep walking.

I needed to leave now, but as I rose, a profound sadness came over me. I didn't want to leave the snug, safe center of the Labyrinth.

Regardless, I began walking the path back. As I walked, joy overwhelmed me and before long I was praising God for His grace. At one point I began singing, "Lord prepare me to be a sanctuary, pure and holy, tried and true."

As I approached the edge of the canvas mat, to step back into the real world, I was both excited and joyful. I knew now why God wanted us to build a Prayer Labyrinth at Cross Roads.

At home, I went straight to the Internet and studied every entry I could find on the subject of labyrinths, amazed at the number of different styles and types. They could be constructed of canvas or garden hedges, or simply outlined in rope or rock. Some were permanent, while others were drawn in sand or dirt and erased when no longer needed.

I ordered books on how to build one. Surely it couldn't be that hard, and we could certainly afford rope, or maybe even rock. The day the books arrived, I opened the package and sat down to absorb whatever I needed to know.

Unfortunately, the secret of the labyrinth was math, not my strong suit, by far. This particular math was called "sacred geometry." Although I studied the books and the equations for several days, I knew it was hopeless.

The right space would have to be located, and an area large enough for a labyrinth would have to be hacked out of the heavy woods. Using rock would make it permanent, but a lot of man or womanpower would be needed to haul the rocks and place them properly.

I talked to God that day in earnest confusion. I knew He wanted a Prayer Labyrinth built at Cross Roads, but once again, He had given me a job to do that seemed impossible. Getting no immediate answer, I despondently shoved the books onto the bookshelf, where they remained untouched until after I married Pat.

Pat's degree is in statistics and mathematics. *Perfect.* I gave him the books and asked him to help figure out the secret. He dutifully read the materials, but once again the books ended up back on the shelf.

Now, after all this time, the idea of building God's Prayer Labyrinth might be possible after all. Not only was Melissa familiar with the subject, because her church possessed one, but the previous summer her pastor, the Reverend Jo Hudson, had traveled the entire southeastern United States learning to build labyrinths. This was the very same person whose grandfather's house I had bought from the Methodist church in Somerville.

A coincidence? I didn't think so. As had happened so often in the past, I felt God's hand guiding me toward what He wanted accomplished.

She enthusiastically volunteered to help with our project and enlisted a mathematician friend of hers who taught alternately at Blinn College in Bryan and the American University in Qatar. They drove out to Cross Roads the following week.

After discussing the different styles and sizes, we decided on a sixty-foot diameter, with fifteen concentric circles or "circuits" outlined in rectangular white limestone. They would create the design and handle the calculations. A materials list would be ready for me within a week. Meanwhile, Melissa would help me locate a good spot for this exciting new addition to Cross Roads.

The following Friday, Melissa and I began our search. Machetes in hand, we probed the woods for an area fairly close to the main camp that would not require a bulldozer to clear it. Translation: no big trees. As always, it was hot, sweaty and slow going through the underbrush.

After we'd been at it for a few minutes, I remembered an area we'd used briefly in the summer of 1997 for a misting meadow. We had hung misting nozzles in the trees to create our version of the misting tents found at summer concerts. The squirrels loved having a tree top water source, so much so that they shredded the hoses.

In the six years since then, the yaupon and greenbrier vines had completely reclaimed the area, catching our clothes and tearing at our hair as we pushed in the direction of the abandoned misting meadow. We eventually located a spot that had one oak and an abundance of smaller yaupon, dogwoods and brush. The growth was so dense that it was hard to tell whether the space would work once it was cleared. We shook our heads, not sure about it at all.

"There's another spot I want to show you across the drive," Melissa said.

As I turned to retrace my steps, she spoke again, almost in a whisper.

"Never mind," she said. "This is where it needs to be."

"We should consider all our options," I reminded her. "Let's see the other spot you have in mind."

"No, Hilda, it has to be here. Turn around and look."

I turned around, but didn't see anything. Then my gaze followed hers up the oak tree to a limb overhanging the center of the space where we were standing. A length of twine was draped over the limb. Attached to one end of the twine dangled the remnants of three popped balloons. On the other end, a piece of brown grocery bag fluttered in the breeze. It had been cut with pinking shears and laminated. Childish writing, in crayon, stated, "I am God."

In the days ahead, the project that had stagnated on my bookshelf for nearly two years slid into the fast lane. We wimped out and hired a local man to clear the area, which he did in less than a day. I ordered rock with the proceeds from a youth group that came from Temple, Texas the next weekend. With the materials and the space ready to go, several men from my church, Pat, my daughter Jennifer, most of my Accountability Group, and a few other women met the following Saturday to build the labyrinth.

Before getting started, we prayed over the new clearing. Then Jo and her friend, Dawn, used short wooden spikes and a tape measure to lay out the fifteen concentric circles. They strung twine from spike to spike, outlining each circle individually.

The rest of us piled load after load of limestone rock into wheelbarrows and "mules" (utility vehicles) and wheeled them along the narrow seventy-five-foot trail to the building site. Placing the stones along the lines of twine was arduous, backbreaking work, but we were many and the task progressed quickly. When all of the circles were lined with limestone, we removed the stakes and twine, and Dawn asked us all to step back.

Thoughtfully and deliberately, she moved from spot to spot to spot, seeing, or sensing, a pattern that was completely invisible to the rest of us. She moved the stones this way and that. Fifteen minutes later, she stood back and, *poof*, there it was, an amazing tree-shaded Prayer Labyrinth.

We had allotted an entire day to complete the job. It took all of two hours.

As we stood around the perimeter, admiring the intricate pattern created by the winding path, you could hear a pin drop.

No one dared speak for fear of spoiling the power of that moment. After a while, Jo broke the silence.

"Let's stand in the center of the labyrinth for a prayer."

Surrounded by the path, snug in the heart of God, we held hands and humbly thanked Him for choosing to use us to accomplish this magnificent purpose. We prayed for Him to bless beyond measure every person whose path led to this sacred place.

The Labyrinth

BEN GRISMER: *The Camp Will Always Move Me*

February 9, 2007

There's a place I think of sometimes, sometimes hot, sometimes cold but always feeling as though the temperature was just right, as though God had said, "I'm turning on the heater" or "I'm turning on the air," and then you thought, "Yeah, I figured You'd make it seventy-four," or "Yeah, ninety sounds good today." The cabins in which we stay (by we I mean myself and the rest of us campers) are small and yet somehow roomy. It never feels cramped, always comfortable, as if we always lived together, as if we'd never left home. The bathrooms are cleaner than the ones at other camps. They're somehow personal, as if they hadn't been used since we were here last year. The meals are always delicious, breakfast, lunch and dinner. The room where we eat served as a game room, too, last year. There's a new room for games now, but the camp still feels the same, always will feel the same, I suppose. I can remember my first time at the obstacle course. I'm still just as terrible at it. I can remember my first snipe hunt there, scaring others into believing in the little nocturnal birds, and I remember Mr. Akers howling and moaning in the bushes, pretending to be a wampus rat, and then slowly rising out of the bushes in a white sheet with a knee pad on his face. I can remember walking the trails out behind the buildings, reflecting on my life while talking to my friends. We found a pond out there and we all lay on the dock, soaking in the sun. I found a half barrel with two by fours nailed to it. I proudly proclaimed, "This is my boat, the Jolly Roger, and I am the pirate Captain Morgan!" Then one of my friends cried out, "Well, if you're a pirate, let's see you sail that ship!" Then I replied, "What? I don't get a loyal crew?" None of them volunteered. I remember one of my friends sinking my "boat" with me still aboard. Somehow, we all managed to end up in the water. I can still feel the water and mud all over me. I remember the first snake I saw there. He didn't seem to care about us. He just sat there enjoying the sunlight. Too bad he was in the middle of our path home. I remember coming back to the pond with the others, pushing the floating dock around the pond with long sticks like gondoliers. I remember my first time in the labyrinth. It's really just a path marked with bricks in a maze-like pattern. I remember shuffling along lost, not in a maze but in prayers and thoughts, lost in the darkness of the surrounding camp and yet found by the candles on the path and the stars in the sky. I remember my second trip to the labyrinth. It was this past year. It was just as moving as the first. I think this camp will always move me, every time I visit, or more like every time I come back home, back home to the perfect weather, the lazy snake, the cold pond, the challenging obstacle course, the cozy cabins, the roaring fires, the spiritual labyrinth and God. The camp is called Cross Roads, and our trip is called a retreat, and when I go I think, "I'm at a crossroads where I can get back on the right path and retreat from everything ungodly." That's really what the trip is for, and I'll never forget.

Ben Grismer, a member of the St. John's Youth Fellowship
This essay was published in the *Rockdale Reporter.*

Now glory be to God, who by His mighty power at work within us is able to do far more than we would ever dare to ask or even dream of - infinitely beyond our highest prayers, desires, thoughts, or hopes. - Ephesians 3:20

CHAPTER 32

The Perfect Spot

Plans for the new conference room had been completed and bids were coming in. Pat spent a few minutes studying them, then set the papers aside and turned the full force of his gaze on me.

"You know, Hilda, it would be cost effective to build the Chapel at the same time we build the conference room."

"Cost effective, with what money? The conference room will take everything we've got."

"Yes, it will take every penny we've raised." He nodded slowly, his eyes probing mine as he continued. "But I want to donate the money for the chapel."

I gasped, as his words registered. His generosity left me speechless, all I could offer was a weak, "Okay, then," as I flung my arms around his neck.

Nine years earlier, when Buddy came out to doze our driveway, I'd asked him to also clear out a notch on the hilltop. That spot was designated as the site for the Cross Roads chapel, which at the time was to be the first building we constructed. As our plans continuously changed, building the chapel became a dream for the future. Scott hung a swing for me on the limb of the oak tree next to the clearing. Sitting there on that swing always reminds me of the camp in South Texas and the moment I first felt God's touch.

At the foot of the hill stands a massive iron ore stone. I found that stone when my brother, John, came to build the porch. It took four men to put the stone in the truck that day and set it at the bottom of the hill. But I insisted. Now, it stands guard, reminding me that God brought me to this place. It's my marker stone. I have spent hours on my swing, planning, dreaming, envisioning the completed camp, and talking with God.

The chapel

Okay, then …

I knew that Pat had been thinking about building the chapel for quite a while. Every time we attended a worship service at a different church or chapel I could see him counting heads, measuring walls, and figuring costs in his mind. He is so quick with numbers that I frequently joke that he's my personal calculator. But now he was treading on sacred ground, planning to design the chapel I had dreamed of for so many years. My defenses flew up.

"I'm not sure the chapel will fit on that spot without more dozer work," he said. "Not if we plan to fill it with a couple hundred people."

"Well, it should. We planned for it when we dozed the site."

"It's better to plan big, scale down later, if necessary. We'll look at it."

The size wasn't our only point of contention. The beauty of cedar siding or the easy maintenance of HardyiPlank? A trendy tin roof or composition shingles that were guaranteed to keep the interior cooler and quieter? A tile floor, carpet, or stained concrete? Square windows? Rectangular? High or low? Agreement did not come easily between us, and after all, it was his money. But it was *my* God given vision.

Finally, we settled on a plan. When the time came to measure the proposed building site, I held the tape measure as Pat unrolled it. We hammered a stake in to set the first corner, then moved to the second, third and fourth. Pat stood back and regarded the space we'd marked out. He raised his eyebrows at me, obviously amazed.

"It will fit perfectly," he admitted.

I tried to keep the "I told you so" out of my smile.

It's Not About ...

Pat had a novel design idea for fashioning a cross over the chancel area. While working on an Epiphany, a spiritual retreat for incarcerated youth at the Giddings State School, he had admired the way the sunlight angled through a high window. He wanted to incorporate a similar feature in the chapel.

The siding went up, the roof went on. As usual, construction moved quickly up to that point, but interior work is tediously slow. First wiring for the lights and sound equipment, then insulation, duct work for the heat and air, sheetrock, flooring …

Finally, Pat climbed on the roof to help three roofers lift an eight-foot cedar cross and slide it into place above the portico. The cross towered over the field, welcoming everyone to Cross Roads. Better than anything I had imagined.

None of the buildings at Cross Roads had turned out the way I envisioned them. Square or rectangular HardiPlank in forest green or tan was attractive nestled among the oaks and yaupon, but a far cry from my dreams of Austin rock and cedar, with tin roofs. I had wanted a rustic chapel with cactus xeriscaping.

But HardiPlank is durable, affordable, and eco-friendly. I believe God appreciates those qualities.

My stepson, Kevin, who had once attended a retreat at the camp, often helped out now.

"You know, looking at the camp, I always thought it was kinda lame," he told me. "But, I get it now. It's a really, really good thing."

I wonder how many times God will have to remind me that it was never about the buildings.

It's About What Happens Here

On February 11th, 2006, I sat on my swing watching cars, trucks, and church vans pull up the drive and park, filling up the field below. Brazos Valley Emmaus members were arriving for a worship service at Cross Roads. People exited their cars and walked toward me, smiling, offering warm greetings and hugs as they made their way up the slope, but my gaze drifted to the western tree line.

I imagined my brother Dale spinning and laughing, exclaiming, "Look! Look! This is it!" as Jennifer, Scott, Nina, Jeremy, J and I popped out from the woods one by one, followed by Jennifer's little brown dog, Ginger. I imagined the long mown waves of grass brushing against my legs now, as they had back then, and the sweet scent of wildflowers hanging in the air. I recalled the wonder of envisioning this blessed place for first time, and now, seeing it as a reality, my heart overflowed with the elation of a dream fulfilled.

Joyful music spilled from the towering double doors, and I joined a crowd of my dearest friends as they took their seats. The polished cedar ceiling vaulted warmly to a peak covering all within protectively. Down each side wall marched tall slender windows, divided by milk glass sconces. At the very front, high up on the wall toward the peak, a magnificent window in the shape of an enormous cross came alive with the beckoning limbs of the trees behind it. Then 180 voices exploded in song, and the Holy Spirit's presence electrified every individual in the room.

I slid into the back row, next to my friends who had worked with me from the beginning. As my gaze swept over the many people I had come to know from Chriesman, Caldwell and Emmaus, I realized how rich I had become in ten busy years, rich with loving friendships and compassionate acquaintances.

Pat circled back and forth around the room taking pictures. I saw him lower the camera for a moment and wipe his eyes, and I knew they were misting at least as much as mine were. Cross Roads had become almost as dear to him as it always had been to me.

I could see the back of Mary's head in the front row, as usual. Carol was still standing, hugging everybody in sight and beaming in the moment. Love radiated from every face, love of Christ, love of each other, love of humanity. God *is* love and God was there. I sat spellbound, humbled beyond belief as I felt the touch of His love and His gratification in this glorious culmination of this stage of our journey together. Waves of relief, release, and incredible joy washed through me. I had worked diligently for Him, and He had come through for me in a big, big way.

A friend leaned over to me, breaking the trance, and said, "Did you ever think you would see this?"

"This is His vision," I said. "It was never about me." He chose to do this God-sized task through me, an unprepared, naïve, unworthy vessel, so that the world could see something happen that clearly only God could accomplish. So many times on this journey, I stood at a new, often unexpected, crossroad wondering where to go next. If I chose wrong, which I often did, God found a way to guide me in the direction He wanted me to go. And on the best occasions, He sent angels to help me along.

Collecting myself, I joined my voice with those of my friends and sang thanksgiving and praises to God from whom *all* blessings flow. All glory to God. Amen

Those who know your name will trust in you, for you, Lord, have never forsaken those who seek you. - Psalms 9:10

AFTERWORD

Beyond the Crossroad

As I write this, it has been fourteen years since the day Nina and I drove out of Houston headed toward our grand adventure. At times it seems like only a moment ago. At other times, when I focus on all that's happened to bring Cross Roads to the vision God gave me that day, it feels as if a lifetime has passed. In some ways, it *was* a lifetime, because I first had to arrive at a place where God could use me to accomplish his mission.

Pat and I continue to explore new ways to make the camp better, but in all the ways that count, it's complete now. I still volunteer as Camp Director and work closely with the manager and weekend volunteers to make sure the hospitality remains "radical." Mostly, I handle the every day details of running a business and booking groups for retreats.

I also serve as Chairman of the Board. None of our seven board members are paid; we're all volunteers. The Board oversees the camp's financing, sets prices, and establishes policies. The one policy that will never change is in regard to the groups we welcome to Cross Roads. This camp will always be open to any group seeking a place to experience God.

The Road Goes On

As Dwight L. Moody said, "It is a masterpiece of the devil to make us believe that children cannot understand religion. Would Christ have made a child the standard of faith if He had known that it was not capable of understanding His words?"

I witnessed firsthand that children crave deeper spirituality and a real and personal relationship with Christ. Sure, any kid enjoys having the sort of fun that comes with the bells and whistles, the zip lines and a lake with a blob, but that's not what they care about at a deep level.

Amazingly, without the distraction of those activities, the kids that come to Cross Roads discover a sense of community. Hanging out with adults who actually listen to them and take their spiritual quest seriously opens their minds as well as their hearts. Like dry sponges, they soak up that affirmation.

Within this book you've seen adults learning from kids. I learn from them continuously. Kids are deep. They're open. They're more willing to explore their spiritually than most adults. Many adults are leery of a deep spiritual experience. After spending hours building the Prayer Labyrinth at Cross Roads, I was amazed when several of the adult volunteers would not walk it. The kids weren't afraid. They readily embraced it.

The vision I've always had for Cross Roads is to provide a space that enables youth to seek and explore a life-changing spiritual experience. If they can feel God's presence at an early age and hang on to that feeling, perhaps they can avoid the confusion and regrettable choices so many of us have lived through. If I can help one child avoid that pain, I will have fulfilled the mission God gave me.

Without the water slides or basketball courts, Cross Roads will continue. We consider our simplicity a plus, as do the kids who have come here. Cross Roads will continue to give them another choice, an unadorned choice, for seeking and hearing His Voice.

Whatever else I do, personally, Cross Roads will always be central to my life's work. I like meeting and serving people, helping them in any way I can to make that connection with God.

Would I do it all again, knowing how hard it would be? Yes, absolutely. The mission God placed on my heart is worth every minute I devote to it. Am I ready to accept another such challenge? I'd have to think a bit, rest up a bit, and pray a bit, then ... absolutely.

What's most important is that Cross Roads continue. Twenty-three of my original 160 acres have been deeded exclusively to Cross Roads, so that it can serve His purpose independent of my involvement. Through me, and through every wonderful, caring, and energetic soul who helped along the way, God has created a unique island of sanctity. I plan to ensure that Cross Roads remains long after I'm gone for Him to make use of in whatever way He deems worthwhile.

Hilda Baker
February 18, 2011

I would like to express my appreciation to everyone who has participated to make Cross Roads a reality.

It was impossible to include every "God thing" that happened on this journey. I have used the signature events that occurred along our path, but there are so many more that I could probably fill another book. The same is true of the people of God who stepped forward during this journey to make it happen. I've tried to include as many as possible, but there are countless others whose help along the way was crucial to God accomplishing His work in bringing Cross Roads to life. Every contribution of time, gifts, witness and prayer was vitally important and greatly appreciated.

And still necessary ...
Please pray that we will be able to keep overhead down through volunteerism and gifts so that we can continue our primary mission of serving youth.

For more information about opportunities available at Cross Roads for retreat experiences or volunteer service, or to support this ministry financially, see our website at:
www.crossroadsretreat.org

Made in the USA
Middletown, DE
11 March 2022

62433748R00146